India's Communal Constitution

This book speaks to debates on law, constitutionalism and the contested terrain of political identity in modern India. Set against the overwhelmingly liberal design of the Indian Constitution, the book demonstrates a tendency in the Constitution and its practice to identify the Indian people in parochial and especially in religious terms. Named India's Communal Constitution, this tendency is illustrated by drawing on constitutional debates and practice as they address religious freedom, personal law, minority rights and the identification of caste groups.

Thus, casting the Constitution and its practice as a field of contestation, the aspiration to define the Indian people as a community of individual citizens is brought face to face with one of its most significant antagonists – the tendency to cast the Indian people as an embodiment of religious communities, which this book examines and details as India's Communal Constitution.

Mathew John is Professor of Law at the Jindal Global Law School, O.P. Jindal Global University, Sonipat, Haryana. This book grew out of his doctoral work at the London School of Economics on the role that law has played in managing and organising religious tensions in South Asia. He works and publishes on issues bearing on public law, constitutionalism, constitutional theory, pluralism and the legal history of modern India.

India's Communal Constitution

Constitution

Law, Religion and the Making of a People

Mathew John

CAMBRIDGE
UNIVERSITY PRESS

Shaftesbury Road, Cambridge CB2 8EA, United Kingdom

One Liberty Plaza, 20th Floor, New York, NY 10006, USA

477 Williamstown Road, Port Melbourne, vic 3207, Australia

314–321, 3rd Floor, Plot 3, Splendor Forum, Jasola District Centre, New Delhi – 110025, India

103 Penang Road, #05–06/07, Visioncrest Commercial, Singapore 238467

Cambridge University Press is part of Cambridge University Press & Assessment, a department of the University of Cambridge.

We share the University's mission to contribute to society through the pursuit of education, learning and research at the highest international levels of excellence.

www.cambridge.org
Information on this title: www.cambridge.org/9781009317757

First published 2023
Reprint 2024

Printed in India by Avantika Printers Pvt. Ltd.

A catalogue record for this publication is available from the British Library

ISBN 978-1-009-31775-7 Hardback

Contents

Acknowledgements

This book is an attempt to answer in some detail a question that has plagued me from as long as I can remember: How is it possible to demarcate the profound diversity of India (perhaps even South Asia) into the clearly demarcated legal and administrative identities we have now come to call Hindu and Muslim? As legally bounded administrative entities, these identities have become important axes along which Indians have been demarcated and walled off from each other. Social experience, however, has always been more complex, and continues even to this day to be porous across these boundaries. Straddling social experience and the straightjacket of administratively organised identities, this book details a Communal Constitution that elaborates law's participation in fastening India and Indians to religious identity.

The problem of religious identity that this book addresses traces back to my doctoral dissertation on the practice of secularism in the Indian constitutional state. Taking forward the dissertation, this book reworks and extends the intellectual journey that began with my doctoral work. Over these years I have accumulated innumerable intellectual debts, some of whom I must explicitly acknowledge.

This book would not have been possible had it not been for Michael Dowdle at the National University of Singapore whose intellectual engagement and generosity made apparent to me that my work on law, religion and Indian constitutionalism could be of interest to a reading public both in India and beyond. Equally there have been many others with whom I have worked with and interacted over the years who have influenced the manner in which this book has come together.

At the National Law School in Bangalore I was introduced to legal study, and especially to the insight that the law was more than just a technical appraisal of rules. In particular I am grateful to Sitharamam Kakarala, who opened out many worlds of enquiry and scholarship in law society and politics. At the Centre for the Study of Culture and Society in Bangalore I got the chance to work with an extraordinary set of scholars who as teachers and colleagues gave me the confidence to think of academic work and scholarship as a profession. Discussions with Ashish Rajyadakshya, Tejaswini Niranjana, S. V. Srinivas and Vivek Dhareshwar have all shaped my understanding of law and religion as a force in modern politics.

At the University of Warwick I had the good fortune to study with the legendary Upendra Baxi. His work has always been an inspiration, especially through the time and insight that he has so liberally made available to his numerous admirers and students like myself. At the London School of Economics my dissertation supervisors Martin Loughlin and W. T. Murphy kept my project on the road even as my own self-belief often flagged. In the years since, Martin's work on constituent power has been a peg around which I have woven the overarching themes that have shaped this book.

This book was finally written up across the time I have spent at two institutions. First, and most importantly, the time I have spent in teaching, learning and researching about Indian constitutionalism at Jindal Global Law School. Second, at the Kate Hamburger Center for Advanced Study in the Humanities in Bonn where I was on a fellowship for a year. Many colleagues at Jindal have extended the warmth of collegiality and also improved the ideas in this book over these years. In particular I would like to thank Pritam Baruah, Sameena Dalwai, Upasana Garnaik, Yugank Goyal, Dipika Jain, Rajeev Kadambi, Mohsin Raza Khan, Gitanjali Surendran, Shivprasad Swaminathan, Faiz Tajuddin, Neha Teyshete, Moiz Tundawala and Fouzia Zafar. I am also particularly grateful to successive batches of Jindal students who took my elective courses on the contemporary history of South Asian constitutionalism. This book has been immeasurably improved by their questions and comments. Leading our efforts at the Jindal Law School, C. Raj Kumar has fostered for myself and my colleagues a vibrant academic community. I cannot thank him enough. At the Kate Hamburger Center I am especially grateful to Werner Gephart, Nina Dethloff and Marta Buchloch for their support for my research and writing while at Bonn.

No writing project is possible without the intellectual and emotional support of friends. For unwavering friendship over the years my thanks to Shahrukh Alam, Pratiksha Baxi, Anuj Bhuwania, Arudra Burra, Sharad Chari, Shraddha Chigateri, Philippe Cullet, Shrimoyee Ghosh, Trisha Gupta, Prashant Iyengar, Subasri Krishanan, Akshay Khanna, Sudhir Krishnaswamy, Lawrence Liang,

Vijay Nagaraj, Arvind Narrain, Siddharth Narrain, Achal Prabhala, Vikram Raghavan, Jawahar Raja, Parvati Sharma, Geetanjali Srikantan and Arun Thiruvengadam.

Towards the final stretch I had some superb research assistance from Ashna Ashesh. Also my editors at Cambridge University Press, Qudisya Ahmed and Anwesha Rana, have calmly and meticulously kept the ball rolling and I have been lucky to have their support and counsel.

Lastly, across the highs and lows of putting this book together, few have had to deal with my roughest edges as have my loving and much forgiving family. My parents-in-law, Ajai and Nalini Singh, have been a source of refuge, especially when I have been with them at their beautiful home in Dehradun. My parents, John Mathew and Elizabeth John, have been my earliest teachers, especially about the value and richness of social diversity that I have tried to address in this book. Finally, Arkaja Singh pushed me to the finish line as I was ready to give up on the project more than once. My thanks is to her above all else.

Introduction

Constitutions are statements of ambition. They are the pathways along which a political community envisions its hopes and aspirations. Over time, constitutions are also maps of failure and frustration. This book identifies one such constitutional failure, which it terms India's Communal Constitution. The Communal Constitution picks out a tendency in the Constitution to cast the identity of the Indian people along religious lines. Needless to say, this tendency gnaws at the heart of Indian constitutionalism, the liberal promise of equal liberties. Therefore, describing the grasp of the Communal Constitution, this book examines the manner it might be best understood alongside the Constitution's aspiration to forge a liberal and secular polity.

Outline of the Problem

To elaborate the communal orientation of the Indian Constitution and the drag it exerts on its liberal goals, a few distinctions and clarifications are useful to kick-start the discussion. In studies on communal tendencies in Indian constitutional politics, a standard point of departure has been the rise of Hindu nationalism over the last century, and especially in the period after the rise of the Ram Janmabhoomi–Babri Masjid dispute.[1] These studies examine the phenomenon of Hindu nationalism in Indian public life and the extent to which it has undermined constitutional commitment to secular ideals. By extension, these studies are a comment on the inability of the broadly liberal and secular consensus embodied in the Constitution to hold its own against its adversaries.

In relation to the rise of religious nationalism, some scholars have suggested that the religious and group-oriented character of Indian society has not been well disposed to liberal secular norms.[2] In turn, it could be argued that these dimensions of Indian society have not facilitated a robust defence of its liberal constitutional state. Whatever stance one takes in relation to these arguments, it is important to note that they seek to explain socio-cultural forces that exert an external influence on constitutional institutions and values. In other words, these arguments on the working of constitutional institutions foreground forces like Hindu nationalist mobilisation as influences that are analytically distinct and largely external to the liberal secular organisation of the Indian Constitution.

The sway of Hindu nationalist mobilisation has never been more pressing on India's liberal constitutional state as parties vowing allegiance to it hold the levers of state power in many parts of contemporary India. However, the communal programme of Hindu nationalism and the extent to which it has been successful in contemporary Indian politics are not directly the subject of this study. On the contrary, this study seeks to isolate aspects internal to the structure and practice of the Indian Constitution that entrenches religious groups and identifies the Indian people through the lens of such groups.

Turning towards the structure and orientation of the Indian Constitution, it is important to distinguish the Communal Constitution from the mere fact that the Indian Constitution is authorised by its people. The people of India are undoubtedly a self-constituted political community, but one that has by and large chosen to design its institutions to emphasise a community premised on the coming together of free and equal citizens.[3] Thus, the Communal Constitution does not merely refer to the default condition of modern politics – the coming together of a people to authorise the state and government.

Further, enunciating the will of the Indian people, there are many constitutional provisions that recognise identities like caste, tribe, religion, minorities, language, region, and so on. Thus, caste and tribe groups are recognised, and special provisions for affirmative action are made for them in various parts of the Constitution; religious denominations are recognised and granted broad powers to manage their affairs in matters of religion; and minorities are recognised and granted special educational and cultural rights. These examples are clearly part of a constitutional scheme that recognises and affirms group identity. However, the recognition of groups and the grant of collective rights per se do not pose the further problem of groups being institutionally asserted and entrenched as embodying the people of India. As communitarian scholars have asserted, the recognition of groups or communities in public life as a valuable aspect of human agency can be justified as consistent with a liberal constitutional culture premised on a composite community of free and equal citizens.[4]

On the other hand, identifying particular groups with the 'people' undermines any political community's effort to articulate itself as free and equal. This is very much the case with the Indian Constitution, especially because of its clearly articulated commitment to found a community of free and equal citizens. However, it is against this background that this book picks out the Communal Constitution as a tendency to identify the Indian people in parochial terms. In this respect it is important to note that the Communal Constitution is not merely presented as an episodic challenge posed to the Constitution's liberal norms. That is, it is not occasional state action that could be revised and corrected. On the contrary, the Communal Constitution points to a structural orientation in the Indian constitutional state.

As a structural feature of Indian constitutionalism, the Communal Constitution subsists in the Indian Constitution despite the overwhelming salience of the Constitution's liberal commitments. In addition, nurtured by socio-political forces such as Hindu nationalism, the Communal Constitution could well be able to displace the Constitution's liberal foundations. It is against this backdrop that this book makes salient its case for the study of India's Communal Constitution.

The Problem of Indian Constitutional Identity

The Communal Constitution has been presented up to this point as the pathological expression of constituent power, or the sovereign authority of the Indian 'people'. However, this pathology is also a broader foundational puzzle for all liberal democratic states. That is, if constitutional authority must be tied to the will of a 'people', then it must follow that these people cannot escape the process of self-formulation by drawing boundaries distinguishing insiders from outsiders, self from others, friends from enemies, and so on. In other words, the sovereign power of the people always leaves open the potential of being articulated in national communal parochial terms.[5]

However, the constituent power of the people is widely understood as a field of power where 'material force is converted into political power, ... a "crowd" is transformed into a "people", and ... a governing regime (i.e., constituted power) is conceived as one that derives its authority from the consent of its subjects'.[6] In other words, the coming together of a 'people' as a political community is presented as a process of rationalisation, persuasion and justification, where brute power could potentially be reorganised and made subject to the limits of law and norms. In Anglo-European liberal democratic societies, the 'people' have set their union into law and rules through the hegemonic normative assumption of a political community of free and equal citizens. Having embraced this liberal political tradition, the Indian Constitution is also founded on the equal liberties of its citizens. However, if this were so, how is it possible to explain a structural orientation in the Constitution to characterise the people in communal terms?

This book addresses this question by presuming that liberal norms are not all-encompassing. That is, even as the commitment to the equal liberty of citizens is hegemonic, it is only one among several contending options that any polity has available to it.[7] It is true that a liberal constitutional order founded on equal citizenship is the dominating influence in global politics. It is also true that equal citizenship has been the dominant influence on Indian constitutional organisation. Even so, contemporary liberal politics has always had many, even if less attractive, rivals.

In the Indian case, alternatives to contemporary liberalism include the belief that the Indian people ought to be defined along the lines of religion, language, regions or even an anti-modern Gandhianism that emphasised the everyday plurality of Indian society. The most powerful of these alternative visions of political community projected India as a land of contending religious communities, the most important of these being the Hindus and Muslims.

In fact, the partition of British India could be viewed as the vindication of this point of view, with Pakistan being carved out as a separate Muslim homeland. Independent India was at great pains to make clear that the assertion of popular sovereignty in its new Constitution would not establish a 'Hindu' mirror of the Pakistani state to govern India's plural society. However, the efforts of the Indian Constitution-makers to constitutionalise a liberal government as the expression of popular sovereignty were set against a long history of colonial state formation as well as anticolonial national mobilisation that drew on and entrenched communal identities. That is, communal identities have been, and continue to be, viable sources of political and constitutional identity in modern India. Consequently, despite the best efforts of the Constitution-makers of contemporary India, the historical weight of communal identities has seeped into the constitutional imagination of the Indian people. This book seeks to trace the imprint of these communal identities on the contemporary

Constitution but primarily limits its enquiry to religion and the role it has played in shaping the identity of the Indian people.

The choice of religion as the primary axis of study helps systematically organise the scope of this book's enquiry. But more importantly, the choice is driven by the fact that religion is by far the most important identity that has shaped Indian constitutional history. The partition of British India is a self-standing event marking the significance of religion for Indian constitutional identity. However, partition was only the culmination of a long process through which religion came to the foreground of Indian constitutional politics. Consequently, the constitutional identity of the Indian people as it has been organised along the axis of religion must be briefly outlined before they are elaborated in the chapters that follow.

Religion and the Contours of the Communal Constitution

The British colonial state in India, as already mentioned, was the historical backdrop against which constitutional imagination in modern India took shape. Consequently, to understand the imprint of religion on Indian constitutional identity, this study foregrounds three axes through which the colonial state drew religion into Indian constituent imagination. These are: first, the adoption of toleration as state practice by the colonial state; second, the movement to reform religion in the nineteenth century; and third, the institutional imagination that framed Indian participation in British government along communal lines in the early twentieth century. Each of these axes is outlined and drawn together as the communal shadow that frames the Indian people and their constitutional identity.[8]

Colonial Toleration

Religion and toleration were always cast as foundational problems for the British government in India from the earliest days of the East India Company's rule in Bengal. From the toleration accorded to personal law systems, through the post-mutiny proclamation by the Crown forbearing Indian religious practices, and right up to the final days of the empire in India, toleration was at the heart of the colonial government's policy towards religion.[9]

In adopting toleration as state policy, the colonial government was doing no more than bringing to India a basic model of government that European societies crafted to address religious and social division. That is, responding to the divisive wars over religion in the sixteenth century, European polities fashioned states where religious freedom and toleration of religious difference formed the normative foundations of political union.[10] It is important to emphasise the normative dimension of the European practice of toleration that regarded toleration as a civic duty exhorting forbearance for practices that were found abhorrent and also obliging state practice to be evenhanded or neutral when confronted with divisive religious questions. Therefore, when faced with the religious diversity of India, it was understandable that a similarly normatively driven toleration formed the primary governmental response of the colonial state.[11]

Normative high-mindedness was of course not the only influence that drove the policy for toleration as there were good pragmatic reasons to tolerate Indian diversity to maintain social stability and avoid costly confrontation. Even so, there is good reason to take serious note of the methodological orientation that normative toleration assumed in colonial India, especially the way it cast religion and religious practice. This methodological orientation is particularly apparent in the pervasive colonial search for the true and axiomatically applicable foundations of Indian religious traditions.[12]

To understand the impulse to seek religious truth as toleration became state policy in India, consider this example from the *Asiatic Journal* on the toleration to be accorded to the practice of Sati:

> [I]t is solely because the burning of widows has its foundation, whether erroneously or not, in the religion of the country, that the British laws do not and ought not to interfere. Infanticide, however, practised in India, has no sanction from any one of its systems of religion, but, on the contrary, is abhorred and repudiated by them all. It is simply a civil act, and is, therefore, cognizable by simply civil or temporal laws; but the burning of widows is a spiritual and religious act (however detestable), and therefore only out of the reach of that code of criminal law which the British nation has permitted itself to impose upon India.[13] (Emphasis in original)

This discussion on Sati demonstrates that the practice secured toleration and immunity from criminal prosecution as the colonial state decided that Sati was part of the axiomatically applicable true foundations of a religious tradition. Infanticide, on the other hand, was not recognised as a religious practice and so was identified as an act that could be criminally prosecuted. The methodological commitment to discover truth can also be seen in the way in which different instances of Sati were distinguished from each other as those true to religious doctrine or axioms and those that were not.[14] In turn, true doctrines or foundations of practices like

Sati were often sought out in religious texts and tied to the religious tradition of a people.[15] Further, it was also assumed in the case of Sati that the practice was part of the religious tradition of the Hindu people, a community different from others classified Muslim, Christian, and so on.

Thus, the search for true religious foundations of a practice like Sati is an important instance illustrating the method and orientation through which the state came to axiomatically and deductively identify religion and demarcate religious communities. However, it is important to emphasise that Sati was only one iconic example that picks out a well-established approach that tolerated religious practice by tying it to the axiomatically applicable truths of a religious community or people. A more far-reaching policy decision that embedded a truth-seeking approach towards religion was Governor General Warren Hastings's Judicial Plan of 1772, which promised to govern Indians identified as Hindus and Muslims according to their respective religious laws.

As considerable scholarship has shown, this act of toleration for the supposed religious laws of their Indian subjects sharpened communal identities by identifying vast swathes of local practice with clearly defined doctrinal truths or axiomatically applicable religious laws.[16] The domain of personal laws and its complexities are independently discussed in Chapter 2 but is mentioned here merely to point to the extent to which toleration pulled together diverse religious practices by emphasising the doctrines or truths that axiomatically identified a religious community. Consequently, even paradoxically, toleration produced sharply defined conceptions of religion and a society divided into religious communities or peoples so recognised by colonial state practice.

Social Reform

In the latter part of the nineteenth century a class of Indians across the subcontinent began to develop a fledgling nationalist consciousness about their collective religious and cultural practices. This assertiveness allowed them the legitimacy to speak on behalf of their fellow countrymen as also to reorganise the unethical contours of Indian religious and social practice.[17] In developing a language to speak for other Indians, nationalists were drawn into a debate both among themselves and with the colonial state on the nature of community in India and the way it might be reformed. What ensued was not just legal engagement with the reform of Indian social practices, but a movement for reform organised along lines of religious communities. This process of reform is the second axis through which this book will demonstrate a constituent imagination that has lent itself to fashioning India as a religiously inflected communal state.

Chronologically, however, the earliest efforts towards social reform were initiated by the colonial state itself through a reorganisation of its deferential approach towards religious practices identified as deserving of toleration. That is, as colonial officials became more confident of their rule in India in the course of the nineteenth century, they argued for the reform of what they deemed to be the ethically and morally deficient aspects of Indian religious practices.

However, drawing again on the example of Sati and its abolition in 1829, it is important to note that the abolition of Sati did not imply any backtracking from the commitment to tolerate as the effort to reform and eventually to ban Sati was argued on grounds of religious truth. That is, an important strand of the argument for abolition drew from the position that Sati had no foundation in the religious canon of the 'Hindu' people. Consequently, abolition was possible without disturbing the commitment to tolerate by re-designating Sati as not obligated by the textual traditions of the Hindus.[18]

However, even as toleration remained a broader current in Indian state practice, there were signs of change in attitudes to Indian religious practices as the nineteenth century advanced. In the broader field of personal law, where vast numbers of religiously inspired practices were axiomatically re-drawn as the textual laws of communities styled Hindus and Muslims, there were signs that state practice was moving away from a simple fidelity to textual legal sources. As scholarship has noticed, the colonial state was forced to confront Indian diversity and the centrality of customary usages in the government of social life.[19]

In a heady confrontation that took place within the colonial establishment in the latter part of the nineteenth century, it was argued by judge James Henry Nelson that the entire textually founded approach to the recognition of personal law ought to be reorganised to emphasise customs alone. Nelson, who will be discussed in greater detail in Chapter 2, argued that the colonial commitment to toleration implied that the relevant object of toleration was a plurality of customs followed by different communities across the country. That is, the object of toleration ought not be practices whose foundations were to be axiomatically found in supposedly canonical texts but customs that could be shown to be practised by particular communities.

By the time Nelson came to emphasise custom in the latter part of the nineteenth century, the centrality of custom was already conceded as a matter of institutional practice in much of Hindu and Muslim personal law. However, there were bounds within which custom was adopted by colonial personal law. That is, the recognition of custom was not the acknowledgement and authorisation of usages as practised by particular social groups but usages that could be rendered axiomatically congruent with the locally authoritative textual traditions of Hindu and Muslim law. In addition, custom also had to be congruent with reason and morality, besides being consistently practised and having antiquity.[20]

However, Nelson seemed to suggest an approach to custom that accepted custom on its own terms as the closely held practices of the diverse subjects of the colonial state. In turn this meant that there ought not to be any automatic presumption that customs stood tied to the broader religiously and axiomatically organised truths of Hindu and Muslim law. However, this suggestion seemed to go one step too far for his colleagues in the colonial establishment.[21] They could accept that customs were relevant in determining and working the relevant personal law but could not accede to the suggestion that they do away entirely with the textual tradition that axiomatically organised the field of personal law into distinct and divided groups of religious people.

Nelson's opinions were predictably committed to oblivion, most notably because of the pushback it received from prominent figures in the colonial establishment. However, the resolution of the debate is an important constituent moment in the history of the colonial state as it affirmed personal law (Hindu law in this episode)[22] as the set of axiomatically applicable rules attaching to and governing a distinct people. That is, Nelson's defeat affirmed a colonial axiom of India as a collection of people best understood as divided by doctrinal and axiomatically applicable truths ascertained and administered by the British state.

This detour into the broader course of personal law in colonial India is evidently significant for the role it played in firming up the identity of the Indian people for colonial state practice. However, it is also significant as these identities formed the contours along which nationalist elites in British India began to speak on behalf of fellow Indians and for the re-making of Indian society. Consequently, drawing on colonially styled accounts of Hindu and Muslim identities, nationalists gradually took over earlier efforts of the British to reform Indian society.

Thus, from the latter part of the nineteenth century and well into the middle of the twentieth century, reform was the communally organised terrain on which nationalist elites opened political ground to speak on behalf of fellow Indians.[23] This history will be elaborated in more detail in later chapters, but for the present discussion it is also useful to link reform as a site of communal identification to a broader process of political and constitutional representation organised by the colonial state along the very same communal identities. In turn, this communally organised form of constitutional representation for Indians is the third axis along which this book will trace communal influences in Indian constituent imagination.

Communal Representation in Colonial India

Political representation for Indians through communally organised separate electorates is the most obviously identifiable instance of communal constitutional imagination in British India. This manner of representation formed part of British efforts to legitimate rule, by gradually increasingly Indian participation in the colonial government. Colonial efforts to present increased Indian participation in government, especially its grandiose assertions that Indian involvement in government was a preparatory step to an eventual handing over of power to Indians, are easily dismissed as disingenuous proclamations in bad faith.[24] This is especially so as the colonial state did not relinquish power to Indians until it was eventually wrested from them by nationalist struggle.[25] Even so, the Indian goal of coming together as a sovereign people with an independent state has been significantly shaped by engagement with the limited forms of representative government in colonial India. Therefore, colonial representation requires careful attention as it has tracked the shape of constitutional identity in independent India.

Fledgling forms of representation for Indians in British government can be traced to the aftermath of the revolt of 1857;[26] however, this process gathered momentum only in the first few decades of the twentieth century. In these years the principal challenge of representing Indian opinion in colonial government was framed by the supposed 'communal problem',[27] or the task of organising representation in government for a society understood to be divided by social, cultural and religious factions. This judgement about Indian society provided the colonial state with justification for its role in India as a pedagogue or mentor who would guide Indians towards political unity.[28] In turn, the obligation to tutor Indian subjects was discharged by organising Indian representation in colonial institutions through a series of constitutional statutes, the most important of which were enacted in 1909, 1919 and 1935.

Colonial representation invited communities to participate and learn the ropes of colonial government as communally divided groups. These groups, Muslims being the foremost among them, were eligible for quotas in colonial legislatures through separate electorates, and later for government jobs. As with toleration and reform, Indian participation in colonial government reified social identities and sharpened the fault lines of social division. In turn, this came in the way of a united nation that the colonial government ironically claimed it wanted to forge and pass on to Indians.

Representation therefore pulled together two kinds of accounts of the peoples of British India: first, as a collection of distinct and divided communities for whom representation would have to be organised, and, second, as a people who could potentially be pulled together to express a sovereign unity, a goal shaped initially by colonial pedagogy and later by nationalist aspiration. The ascendance of the Indian national movement, and the eventual adoption of the Indian Constitution, was of course an effort in moving past the colonial logic that Indians could only express themselves as communities. However, community, especially religion, continues to exert constituent force on the design and practice of the Constitution of independent India.

Communal representation gathered within its fold a range of identities that the colonial state saw important to represent in Indian government. Religious groups, especially Muslims, were only one of the groups that were recognised by the scheme of colonial representations. Other represented communities included caste groups, property groups, regional groups, and so on. Nonetheless, religious communities, and Muslims in particular, were a significant communal group that found recognition under the scheme of communal representation to emerge on the Indian political stage in the first half of the twentieth century.

As already mentioned, the creation of Pakistan as a Muslim homeland was a clear indication of the strength of religion as a constituent force in British India. By contrast, the Indian Constitution was intended as a repudiation of the colonial judgement that India could be no better than a conglomeration of parochial communities. However, as the following chapters will demonstrate, there are elements of a colonially and in particular a religiously organised conception of the Indian people that have passed into the Indian Constitution.

Thus, to sum up the efforts of this section, conceptual accounts of toleration, social reform and communal representation have been pulled together as constituent axes making for a communal and religious organisation of the peoples of British India. It must of course be emphasised that neither this chapter nor indeed this book is intended to be a detailed historical elaboration of these axes of constituent imagination in colonial India. On the contrary, this conceptual framework is only an analytical frame that recasts existing scholarship to account for the forms in which colonial institutions and conceptual categories organised along communal lines continue to leave an imprint on the liberal Constitution that India adopted at independence. This imprint of the colonial state on contemporary India will be detailed in the following chapters even as the next section outlines that broader effort.

The Independence Constitution as a Communal Constitution

Mapping the communal imprint of colonial constitutional imagination on the Constitution of independent India is no easy task. The task is made no easier even when religion is the only vantage through which the Communal Constitution is examined. This is because there are many sites on which the colonial conceptualisation of India as a religious people maps onto contemporary constitutional design and practice. These include, for example, the practice of free speech law in ways exceptionally solicitous to religious sentiments, laws on religious institutions that have required and permitted active state supervision, the recognition of cow protection as a goal that the new republic must strive to achieve, or even citizenship laws that have been less than neutral to individuals (mostly Muslim) who sought to come to India from neighbouring countries.

Many of these aspects of Indian constitutional practice are likely candidates to study the communal legacy of the colonial state passed onto the contemporary Constitution. However, these aspects of constitutional organisation and practice are only peripherally addressed by this book. By contrast this book will contour the Communal Constitution through chapters on the constitutional organisation and adjudication of religious freedom, personal law, minority rights and the identification of caste groups. The choice of these areas of constitutional organisation and practice is partly ad hoc but also motivated by the understanding that the broader scope of these debates makes them candidates better suited to demonstrate the emphasis of communal identity in the Indian Constitution and its practice.

Before a discussion of the chapters themselves, it is useful to foreground two methodological moves that pull together the Communal Constitution across the following chapters. First, each chapter maps continuities between the Constitution of independent India and that of the colonial state that preceded the contemporary Constitution. Second, the chapters also draw on these constitutional continuities to demonstrate the entrenchment of doctrinally, scripturally or axiomatically organised religious identities as embodiments of the Indian people. Collectively, these methodological moves pull the chapters of this book together as interlocked debates that make salient a communal constitutional sensibility.

Accordingly, Chapter 1 begins its discussion of religious freedom by detailing the 'essential practices test', a legal doctrine that the Indian Supreme Court has deployed to delimit religious freedom. The doctrine has identified religious freedom by granting judges considerable hermeneutic power to interpret and establish religious doctrines of religious communities. Scholars have identified this approach to religious freedom as weighing against the secular liberal aspirations of the Indian Constitution. However, bracketing normative enquiry on the appropriateness of the doctrine for constitutional interpretation, this chapter traces the continuing trust that courts have placed in the essential practices test to demonstrate the historical weight of colonial toleration on the determination of essential religious practices. In addition, through a detailed examination of the Ram Janmabhoomi–Babri Masjid dispute, the chapter illustrates an extreme instance through which the essential practices test has organised religious freedom to entrench the communal character of the Indian people understood as Hindu and Muslim. Contrasting approaches emphasising liberal, secular and non-communal values of the Indian Constitution have always been available to the Indian courts to resolve problems associated with religious freedom. Nonetheless, the scriptural and hermeneutic method of the essential practices test has organised religious freedom by foregrounding the communal truth of particular religious traditions. In doing so, the chapter argues, the essential practices test has emphasised religious communities and the differences between them as the fault lines that have played up the identities of the Indian people.

Chapter 2 extends the account in Chapter 1 to demonstrate the manner in which axiomatically organised scriptural conceptions of religious community are reinforced by the Indian constitutional practice of personal law. It is possible to view personal law solely as an instance of constitutionally recognised group rights. However, adopting an unusual approach to personal laws, a strand of Indian constitutional practice has recognised personal laws as scripture immune to constitutional scrutiny, especially of fundamental rights. Through this strand of constitutional practice, Chapter 2 foregrounds a constituent imagination illustrating a scripturally and communally founded conceptualisation of the Indian people in the organisation and practice of personal law.

Chapters 3 and 4 explicitly shift the orientation of the book towards Indian constitutional design and its conception of its people. Doing so, these chapters explore the manner in which the Constitution draws on scripturally, doctrinally, and axiomatically organised religion to entrench a communal conception of the Indian people. Historically this aspect of Indian constitutional design traces its origins to colonial efforts facilitating political representation for Indians in the nineteenth and twentieth centuries – that is, through institutional mechanisms such as separate electorates which drew Indians into British government along the lines of their communally ascribed affiliations. Accommodating Indians in colonial government by way of their communal identities continues to have echoes in the design and practice of minority rights and the identification of caste groups, which are detailed in Chapters 3 and 4 respectively.

Both Chapters 3 and 4 detail the way constitutional practices identify minorities and castes by casting them as nationalised and axiomatically organised scriptural entities. Other forms of identifying both minorities and castes can plausibly be asserted even up to the present day. However, constitutional design and practice have been predisposed to identifying minorities against the backdrop of a axiomatically and scripturally organised Hindu majority, and castes solely as constituent elements in a Hindu scriptural order. As these chapters detail, the constitutional criteria to identify minorities could just as easily pick out sub-groups from among those currently recognised as Hindus. Similarly, the sociological criteria that identifies Scheduled Castes, with whom the Constitution makes a special compact, could also isolate castes among many 'non-Hindu' groups. However, the commitment to a communal constitutional imagination does not allow these alternative possibilities. Consequently, constitutional debates on caste identification and minority rights reiterate axiomatically and scripturally founded conceptualisations of a Hindu community and, along with it, the Communal Constitution that this book seeks to spotlight. The contours of this Communal Constitution and the challenge it poses to India's liberal constitutional aspirations are detailed in the chapters that follow.

Notes

1. For a recent example, see Angana P. Chatterji, Thomas Blom Hansen and Christophe Jaffrelot (eds.), *Majoritarian State: How Hindu Nationalism Is Changing India* (London: C Hurst & Co Publishers Ltd, 2019).

2. For example, T. N. Madan, *Modern Myths, Locked Minds: Secularism and Fundamentalism in India* (2nd edn, New Delhi: Oxford University Press, 2009).

3. For a recent defence of this position, see Madhav Khosla, *India's Founding Moment: The Constitution of a Most Surprising Democracy* (Cambridge, MA: Harvard University Press, 2020).

4. For a classic statement of this position, see Will Kymlicka, *Liberalism, Community and Culture* (Oxford: Oxford University Press, 1989).

5. See Martin Loughlin, 'On Constituent Power', in *Constitutionalism beyond Liberalism*, ed. Michael W. Dowdle and Michael A. Wilkinson, 151–75 (Cambridge, UK: Cambridge University Press, 2017).

6. Loughlin, 'On Constituent Power', 151–52.

7. For a related articulation of constitutionalism as a site of contestation, see Upendra Baxi, 'Constitutionalism as a Site of State Formative Practices', *Cardozo Law Review* 21 (1999): 1183–210.

8. These axes recast an extensive corpus of scholarly writing. Some examples include Jakob De Roover and S. N. Balagangadhara, 'Liberty Tyranny and the Will of God: The Principle of Toleration in Early Modern Europe and Colonial India', *History of Political Thought* 30, no. 1 (2009): 117–25; Pratap Bhanu Mehta, 'Hinduism and Self-Rule', *Journal of Democracy* 15, no. 3 (2004): 108–21; Partha Chatterjee, *The Nation and Its Fragments* (New Delhi: Oxford University Press, 1995); Reginald Coupland, *Report on the Constitutional Problem in India: The Indian Problem, 1833–1935* (Oxford: Oxford University Press, 1943).

9. See, for example, Donald Eugene Smith, *India as a Secular State* (Princeton: Princeton University Press, 1963).

10. John Rawls, *Political Liberalism* (New York: Columbia University Press, 2005), xxiv.

11. See De Roover and Balagangadhara, 'Liberty Tyranny and the Will of God', 111.

12. De Roover and Balagangadhara, 'Liberty Tyranny and the Will of God', 117–25.

13. De Roover and Balagangadhara, 'Liberty Tyranny and the Will of God', 122.

14. Lata Mani, 'Contentious Traditions: The Debate on Sati in Colonial India', in *Recasting Women: Essays in Indian Colonial History*, ed. Kumkum Sangari and Sudesh Vaid, 88–126 (New Delhi: Kali for Women, 1989).

15. Mani, 'Contentious Traditions'.

16. For example, Bernard S. Cohn, 'Law and the Colonial State in India', in *Colonialism and Its Forms of Knowledge: The British in India* (Princeton: Princeton University Press, 1996); Richard W. Lariviere, 'Justices and Panditas: Some Ironies in Contemporary Readings of the Hindu Legal Past', *The Journal of Asian Studies* 48, no. 4 (1989): 757; Michael Anderson, 'Islamic Law and the Colonial Encounter', in *Institutions and Ideologies: A SOAS South Asia Reader*, ed. David Arnold and Peter Robb, 165–85 (London: Routledge, 1993); Manan Ahmed Asif, *The Loss of Hindustan: The Invention of India* (Cambridge, MA: Harvard University Press, 2020).

17. For a classic account of this moment, see Chatterjee, *The Nation and Its Fragments*.

18. Mani, 'Contentious Traditions'.

19. A classic instance illustrating this change is the Privy Council decision in *Collector of Madura v. Mootoo Ramalinga* 12 M.I.A. 397 (1868).

20. Geetanjali Srikantan, *Identifying and Regulating Religion in India: Law, History and the Place of Worship* (New Delhi: Cambridge University Press, 2020).

21. L. C. Innes, *Examination of Mr. Nelson's Views of Hindu Law, in a Letter to the Right Hon. Mountstuart Elphinstone Grant Duff, Governor of Madras* (Madras: Higginbotham & Co., 1882).

22. The Nelson episode only foregrounds the way the colonial state dealt with the problem of custom in relation to Hindu law. However, a similar account could be made of Muslim law as well, especially the inability of custom to displace the centrality of the textual tradition.

23. See Partha Chatterjee, 'Secularism and Tolerance', in *Secularism and Its Critics*, ed. Rajeev Bhargava, 345–79 (New Delhi: Oxford University Press, 1999).

24. See, for example, Rohit De, who dismisses these colonial intentions as part of a whiggish conception of history. Rohit De, 'Constitutional Antecedents', in *The Oxford Handbook of the Indian Constitution*, ed. ed. Pratap Bhanu Mehta, Madhav Khosla and Sujit Choudhry, 17–38 (New Delhi: Oxford University Press, 2016).

25. Chatterjee, *The Nation and Its Fragments*, 14–35.

26. See Sarvepalli Gopal, *British Policy in India, 1858–1905* (Cambridge, UK: Cambridge University Press, 1965).

27. For example, see Coupland, *Report on the Constitutional Problem in India*.

28. Coupland, *Report on the Constitutional Problem in India*.

The Communalisation of Religion in Indian Constitutional Law

This chapter begins the task of charting the communal identification of the Indian people in the constitutional practice of religious freedom. It does so by drawing on a genealogical account of toleration and the movement to reform religious practices in colonial India as they have determined the contours of religious freedom in the Indian Constitution. Doing so, this chapter also sets out the methodological approach through which this book makes salient the forms in which colonial state practice communally inflects contemporary constitutional design and practice.

Outlines of the Constitutional Scheme Regulating Religion

To make apparent the form in which the government of religion by the Indian Constitution communally inflects the identity of the Indian people, it is important to begin by outlining the contours along which the Constitution seeks to regulate religion and religious freedom in particular. The obvious place to begin this task would be the provisions on religious freedom which are laid out in a set of four constitutional provisions in the chapter on fundamental rights (Articles 25–28). Between them, these provisions protect the right to religious freedom for individuals and groups, provide for state action against religion in the public interest, and specifically mention instances where the state and religious power ought not to impose themselves on an unwilling public. These provisions would seem like those of any liberal constitution.

Therefore, uncovering a communal dimension from these broadly liberally inclined provisions requires deeper scrutiny of their structure and practice.

Of the provisions spanning Articles 25–28, Articles 27 and 28 deal with very particular concerns bearing on the power of the state to impose religious taxes (Article 27) and the bar on religious instruction in educational institutions run on state funds (Article 28). Important as these constitutional guarantees might be, they have not determined the course of religious freedom in the Indian Constitution. On the other hand, Articles 25 and 26 have been key provisions that have determined the template that has come to organise state power as it has been exercised over religion.

Examining these provisions in greater detail, Article 25(1) is structured like a standard liberal freedom where the right to practise, profess and propagate religion is granted to all individuals. However, this provision is subject to other provisions of the fundamental rights chapter and a proviso which permits the state to impose restraints on religious freedom in the interest of public order, morality and health. In addition, Article 25(2) permits the state to 'regulate or restrict economic, financial, political or other secular activity which may be associated with religious practice' (Article 25(2)(a)) and 'provide for social welfare and reform or the throwing open of Hindu religious institutions of a public character to all classes and sections of Hindus' (Article 25(2)(b)).

Sub-clauses (a) and (b) in Article 25(2) clearly provide distinct grounds for the exercise of state power over religion though constitutional practice, especially constitutional adjudication, has understood these clauses as analogous and as extensions of each other. However, even if constitutional interpretation were to develop a more fine-tuned classification of these clauses, they are both organised to empower state action to reform and regulate religious practice. Moreover, these clauses facilitating the exercise of state power over religion is clearly distinct from the more easily recognised restrictions that liberal democracies impose on religious freedom in public interest as laid out in Article 25(1). Of course, state action in public interest can also be seen as empowering the state to act as needed to secure public order, morality, and so on.[1] Even so, the explicit empowerment of state-led reform and regulation of religion in Article 25(2) has pushed it to the centre of discussions pertaining to the institutional design and practice of religious freedom in the Indian Constitution.

Doctrinally and as a matter of constitutional interpretation, the principal problem that Article 25(2) poses is the challenge of delimiting the power that the state can legitimately wield over religious practice. This problem of the legitimate exercise of state power breaks up into three broad questions as it has arisen in the interpretation of Article 25 as also of related provisions of Article 26: First, to what extent does Article 25(2) control 25(1)? Second, to what extent does Article 25(2) control Article 26? Third, and though not directly related to the scope of state power in Article 25(2), to what extent is Article 26 controlled by the other provisions of the chapter on fundamental rights?

To address these questions in turn, it is clear from the text of the Constitution that the power to reform and regulate religion in Article 25(2) overrides and controls the freedom to religious practice granted in Article 25(1). In addition, it must also be reiterated that the right to religious freedom granted to individuals in Article 25(1) is also subject to state control in the interest of public order, morality and health, as well as other provisions of the fundamental rights chapter of the Constitution. However, Article 25(2) sits in some tension with Article 26, a provision that grants denominations the right to manage their religious affairs.

Unlike the freedom in Article 25, which is explicitly subject to a range of restraints as already noted, Article 26 is only subject to the restraints of public order, morality and health. This has raised questions about the extent to which Article 26 is subject to Article 25(2) as well as other fundamental rights. Regarding the tension between Articles 25(2) and 26, the Supreme Court has held that denominational rights to manage religious affairs are subject to the reform and regulatory power of the state under Article 25(2).[2] An allied and related question pertains to the extent to which denominations in Article 26 are subject to the exercise of state power to advance broader constitutional values, especially those embodied in constitutional provisions protecting equality and dignity. This is a problem of interpretation that is unresolved in constitutional adjudication with evidence pointing in different directions.[3]

These questions on the scope of state power across Articles 25 and 26 have in turn been tied to the way constitutional practice has defined and valued religion as a domain that states ought not to violate. The Constitution says very little about the contours of religious freedom, and therefore delimiting the scope of religious freedom has required courts to devise principles for constitutional interpretation. Consequently, examining judicial labours towards this end, this chapter highlights the way constitutional interpretation has functioned to foreground communal identities.

Adjudicating Religious Freedom in the Indian Constitution

For constitutional adjudication, the challenge of delineating the domain of religious freedom against the legitimate exercise of state power has been the identification of 'essentially religious' doctrines, rituals or practices which the state ought not to violate. This interpretative framework wrought by the Supreme Court to identify what is 'essentially religious' has come to be called the 'essential practices test' or the 'essential practices doctrine'.[4]

In its defining decision on the essential practices test, the Indian Supreme Court was called to decide on the constitutional validity of the Madras Hindu Religious and Charitable Endowments Act, 1951.[5] The petitioner in this case, the chief religious functionary of the Shirur Mutt at Udupi, contended that this Madras statute, which granted the government power to take over mismanaged Hindu religious institutions as a trustee, violated the denomination's right to religious freedom and to manage religious institutions as permitted by Article 25(1) and Article 26 of the Constitution. Countering the claims of the petitioner, the state contended that it had the broadest powers of reforming and regulating all 'secular' aspects related to a religious tradition under Article 25(2).

Resolving these contending positions, the Supreme Court devised the essential practices test which continues to guide the determination of constitutionally protected aspects of religious freedom. Addressing the contending arguments in this case the court held that

> ... *what constitutes the essential part of a religion is primarily to be ascertained with reference to the doctrines of that religion itself* ... and the mere fact that they involve expenditure of money or employment of priests and servants or the use of marketable commodities would not make them secular activities. (Emphasis added)[6]

In this manner the court began the search for essential religious practices by seeking out doctrines and practices that a community subjectively viewed to be essential to their religion.

Following *Shirur Mutt*, early Supreme Court decisions seemed relatively open to serious consideration of a community's subjective assertions about their traditions. Thus, in the *Venkataramana Devaru* case,[7] dealing with the claims of the Gouda Saraswath Brahmins that their religious tradition required exclusion of certain communities from certain parts of their temple, the court found in their favour. However, the court held that this denominational right granted by Article 26 to manage affairs in matters of religion was to be balanced with the power of the state to reform such practices in Article 25(2). Accordingly, even as the religious freedom of the Gouda Saraswaths was construed broadly, their denominational rights were held to be subject to the reforming demands of temple-entry legislation which mandated that all Hindu public temples could not exclude any class or section of Hindus.

In the 1960s, however, the strongly statist and reforming orientation of Justice Ganjendragadkar led the Supreme Court to fundamentally transform the essential practices test as it was articulated in the *Shirur Mutt* case. Through a series of decisions,[8] the understanding of essential practices was recast by the Supreme Court from practices a community ascertained as essential to its religious tradition to practices a court judged to be essential to that tradition.[9] This interpretative move opened space for subsequent courts to involve themselves in the resolution of hermeneutic questions associated with the doctrines and practices of various religious traditions. Thus, following Justice Gajendragadkar's lead, the Supreme Court in subsequent decisions has, almost as theologians, sifted between different kinds of religious claims, establishing some while denying others.

To take some examples – the Supreme Court has held that the sacrifice of cows did not constitute an essential part of the Islamic faith;[10] overruled Muslim claims that prayer in a mosque was crucial to the Islamic faith;[11] refused to accept traditional rights of the Tilkayats of the Shrinathji temple at Nathdwara which was taken from them by the Nathdwara Temple Act, 1959;[12] stipulated that the *tandava* dance was not a significant part of the Anand Margi community;[13] declared that the followers of Aurobindo did not constitute a distinct religion;[14] that the tradition of *santhara*, or ritual suicide, did constitute a part of the Jain religion,[15] and so on.

Each of these decisions exemplifies a peculiar form of public reasoning where the judiciary legitimates state regulation and reform through forms of religious interpretation internal to that religious tradition. In so doing courts have not only transformed the essential practices test as articulated in *Shirur Mutt* but also arrogated to itself the last word on what constitutes the essential religious truths of particular religious traditions. Most importantly, it is noteworthy that this transformation was effected without formally overruling *Shirur Mutt*, which continues to be the stated source of the courts' power to determine essential religious practices.

A whole body of scholarship has responded to this manner of governing religion, arguing that it sits uneasily with India's secular constitutional state.[16]

It is not difficult to see why this is the case as this hermeneutic model does not seem to be consonant with the freedoms of individuals and groups to practise religion without fear or prejudice. Of course there could be various models of secular intervention in matters pertaining to religious practice. For instance, religious freedom could be delimited through interpretative frames similar to that adopted in the *Shirur Mutt* case. Alternatively, courts could even adopt models of interpreting the bounds of state power that are less solicitous of religious freedom and which demand religious freedom be firmly justified against the background of other constitutional values such as equality and dignity.[17] Such 'secular' models of regulating religion would also require the state to perform boundary-marking functions between religious freedom and the legitimate and legally permissible bounds of state power. However, even granting such boundary marking, it is difficult to envisage that such secular and liberal constitutional practice could permit courts to substitute their judgment for that of a practitioner or a denomination as is the case with the existing form of the essential practices test.

The line of Supreme Court decisions that have staked out a new approach to essential religious practices since the 1960s does seem to present an incorrect account of the constitutional guarantees on religious freedom. However, mere assertion of error cannot account for the court's resolute affirmation of this incorrect normative position in case after case. That is, judicial error or its inability to live up to constitutional norms does not explain an attachment to error. This section therefore suggests that this error is an opportunity to diagnose the condition made ripe for judicial engagement in religious hermeneutics to determine essential religious practices.

Therefore, in contrast to normative analysis that attempts to evaluate the essential practices test against the text and the values of the Constitution, the following sections attempt to locate the essential practices test against the sweep of socio-historical and political scholarship on the governance of religion in India. Doing so they argue that the essential practices test draws on colonial state practice even as it seems a taint or an aberration on the normative scheme of the Indian Constitution.

The historical antecedents to which this chapter will turn, toleration and social reform, have already been outlined in the introductory chapter as elements of the constituent axes that have determined Indian constitutional identity. The links between these constituent axes are further detailed in the next sections and tied up to the constitutional organisation and practice of religious freedom, especially the hermeneutic approach to essential religious practices. Consequently, by drawing out these connections between toleration, social reform and the essential practices test, this chapter moves the trajectory of its argument towards the communalisation of Indian constitutional identity.

Toleration, Reform and the Regulation of Religion in Modern India

Drawing essential practices from the historical arc of toleration and social reform in India requires a short account of these modalities of government as they have organised religion in modern India. Accordingly, these modes of colonial and contemporary government are detailed in turn, especially as they bear on the hermeneutic model of determining essential religious practices adopted by the Indian Supreme Court.

What Kind of Toleration?

Toleration is the root model through which modern liberal democracies organise state power to govern religious and cultural division. As scholars have shown, the institutionalisation of toleration is founded on the equal protection of individual liberty and is closely tied to the founding of modern politics in all North Atlantic societies. That is, equal liberty of private citizens within a broadly neutral state provided North Atlantic polities with a model to organise stable societies by defanging irreconcilable conflict between religious factions that threatened the prospect of political unity.[18]

Toleration and the commitment to equal liberties, as outlined earlier in this chapter, are clearly also a part of the Indian Constitution. At the same time, it is important to note that the adoption of toleration as value choice precedes the Constitution and is a policy with considerable vintage in the colonial state.[19] However, the adoption of toleration as state policy in the colonial state did not result in an emphasis on individual liberty and the withdrawal of controversial matters of faith from a neutral public sphere. On the contrary, toleration in colonial India only deepened state involvement in religion through a thorough-going search for the religious truths or foundational axioms governing religious practices of their colonial subjects.

Drawing on the history of toleration in European societies, the privatised faith that toleration carved out as a matter of constitutional practice was possible in Europe because it coincided with the changes brought about by the

Protestant reformation, which laid emphasis on individual conscience and the personalisation of faith. As this form of social discipline was absent in India, a government driven by toleration was obliged to deploy state power to foster a landscape that mapped and reordered society along the religious truths of its unreconciled subjects. This effort of mapping the myriad practices of the Indian people to supposed religious truths or axioms has already been outlined in the introductory chapter as the methodological orientation with which toleration operated in colonial India.

The methodological approach of toleration that the introductory chapter has made salient has been alternatively characterised as driven by the prism of expedience and the pragmatic demands of stabilising rule over a diverse society, the expression of colonial control and power, or simply the expression of the insatiable colonial urge to classify and organise the diverse society it came to rule.[20] While there is an element of truth to these claims, it does not capture the normative dimension to toleration. That is, these alternative approaches do not explain toleration understood as an expression of forbearance for practices that were abhorrent, especially those like Sati which strained the ethical and religious commitments of most colonial officials. This aspect of toleration is key to understanding the uniqueness of the concept, especially as it has become the kernel of modern liberal democratic societies both in India and elsewhere.

In an essay that shapes the form in which this chapter deploys toleration as a normative idea, Balagangadhara and De Roover trace the normative aspect of toleration to protestant theological ideas of the inviolate relationship between divine truth and individual conscience which states came to view as values they were bound to respect. More importantly, these scholars show that this inviolate relationship between divine truth and human conscience was also mirrored in India as the early colonial state devised its form of governing the religious practices of its subjects. Thus, it is the normative charge in toleration as a concept that pushed the colonial government to map European forms of organising society onto the Indian religious landscape. Most importantly, as these truths were not readily apparent or available for state policy, the colonial state set up an extensive programme to generate, classify and systematise these truths. As an important pillar of colonial state policy towards religion, this search for the religious truth as state practice must be discussed in greater detail, especially its consequences for the framing and firming of religion and religious identity.

Toleration as Truth Seeking

As a long-standing policy, instances of toleration dot the history of the British colonial state in India from the conquest of Bengal to the transfer of power after Indian independence. Arguably, one of the most important aspects of colonial policy which exemplified the ethic of toleration was laid out in the judicial plan for Bengal in 1772, stating that

> in suits regarding Inheritance, Marriage, Cast, and other religious usages or institutions, the laws of the Koran with respect to the Mahometans, and those of the Shaster with respect to Gentoos, shall be invariably adhered to: on all such Occassions, the Moulavies or Brahmins shall respectively attend to expound the Law, and they shall sign the Report and assist in passing the Decree.[21]

As evident, this assurance given by Governor General Hastings committed the colonial state to tolerate and administer their subjects understood broadly as Hindus and Muslims, each according to their respective religious or personal laws.

Driven by their commitment to tolerate these laws, the colonial state soon found itself drawn into the project of finding and expounding these religious injunctions that they believed governed the lives of their largely Hindu and Muslim subjects. As already described, this state-propelled search for the true religious foundations of personal laws was not just the pragmatic accommodation of the beliefs of a subject population but a norm to which the colonial state had bound itself. The systematisation of personal laws into foundational rules governing distinct religious communities is a topic of much scholarly debate and is addressed in greater detail in Chapter 2 of this book. By contrast, this section contours colonial toleration with broad brush strokes, tying the obligation to tolerate with the making of a communal conceptualisation of the Indian people.

This section does not and cannot offer a detailed account of toleration as it developed and evolved in the colonial state.[22] On the contrary, it merely draws on existing scholarship to elaborate the transformation that colonial toleration brought about in the organisation of religious practice and religious self-understanding. To do so it echoes and amplifies earlier discussions in this book on the iconic instance of Sati as it was subject to colonial government reform and eventually to abrogation.

Historical work on Sati, or wife burning, shows that the early regulation of the practice assumed that it was a practice sanctioned by the Hindu religion. By implication, it followed that the true doctrinal foundations of the practice were to be found in Hindu religious texts and that Hindus were obliged to follow the axioms or doctrinal truths laid out in these texts. Practice was hardly as straightforward as there were no generally applicable texts or axiomatic principles that declared Sati to be a religious practice and many texts that had something of a bearing on whether and how a Sati was to be performed.[23] Further, there was considerable regional variation in the performance of Sati making it unclear whether the practice was applicable to all castes and groups of Hindus as it was presumed. Even so, driven by the normative will to tolerate, colonial courts narrowed on a set of texts that were identified as axiomatic doctrines which formed the basis of the effort to regulate Sati as a Hindu religious practice. Consequently, based on these texts and the interpretative frames that grew around them, Satis were distinguished between those that were scripturally sanctioned and performed with the consent of the immolated women (the good Satis) and those that were not scripturally so recognised (the bad Satis).[24]

This summary account of the debate on Sati reveals the commitment of colonial toleration to identify and protect doctrinally true Satis quite like how the contemporary Supreme Court divines essential practices of various religious denominations. More importantly, axiomatic doctrinal truths identified by state practice pulled together varied practices of diverse communities as the foundational truths of one religious group – the Hindu people. This orientation of the colonial state to tolerate true practice was mirrored in other Hindu practices, as well as with the practices of other communities it came to identify as Muslims, Christians, and so on.[25] In turn this resulted in the conceptualisation of British India as a collection of sharply demarcated religious people or even nations, which will be elaborated in this and subsequent chapters.

Significantly, this conceptualisation of India did not just remain figments of British imagination about their colonial subjects. On the contrary, British conceptualisations of India were internalised by Indians as they began to participate in the structures of British government. Social reform is one such axis along which Indians internalised British conceptualisation of Indian identity, which must now be briefly outlined.

Toleration and the Organisation of Social Reform

Staying with the example of Sati, as the nineteenth century wore on, changing British opinion about the practice created a crisis in Bengali society. That is, increasing British engagement with Sati and with available textual sources gradually unsettled the consensus that the practice was founded on Hindu scriptural sources. This changing official position contributed to a contentious debate in Bengali society, resulting in influential sections of local Bengali society either endorsing or opposing the revised British position that Sati had no religious foundation. Overall, these highly charged debates on Sati allowed the colonial state to press for reform and eventually to ban the practice in 1829.[26]

The abrogation of Sati did not imply the abandonment of the official commitment to tolerate but only a change in the recognition accorded to Sati as a practice embodying the doctrinal truth of the Hindus. That is, the colonial state moved towards the position that there was insufficient scriptural support for the practice and hence that the practice could safely be banned. Significantly, this position was endorsed by a section of the native society on the very same grounds. Even those sections of Bengali society that opposed the ban on Sati did so on scriptural grounds, arguing that the practice was scripturally sanctioned and had religious foundations.[27] Thus, it is possible to understand the ban on Sati not just as the abrogation of the practice but also as the form in which religion would be understood in public debate. That is, the practice of Sati was to be measured against the scripturally enjoined, and axiomatically applied truths of the people identified as Hindu.

This manner of addressing religious practice formed part of a generic and consistent official outlook, though it underwent some degree of change as the nineteenth century progressed, especially in relation to customary practices of local groups. That is, emphasising the importance of customs, religious practices were identified as customary to specific local groups, a development in colonial policy that will be discussed in greater detail in Chapter 2. However, this did not fundamentally disturb the broad contours of linking religious practices with the axiomatic or essential truths of the Indian people nationally identified as Hindu and Muslim, and so on.

Significantly, by the end of the century, Indian nationalists had deeply internalised this colonial approach to framing religious identity. Consequently, when they sought to fashion their legitimacy to speak on behalf of fellow Indians, they did so through social reform projects that were organised along pan-national religious lines. That is, arguing that many traditional and ethically degenerate practices in Indian society required sweeping reform, they made their case to speak on behalf of fellow Indians by reinforcing their identities as Hindu and Muslim people. This process of reorganising practices understood as embodiments of the truths of a people began of course with British efforts to reform and abrogate Sati in the early part of the nineteenth century. However, by the end of the century, as nationalist sentiment began to gather force, Indian elites assumed the lead on reform by relegating the role of the colonial state to the margins. Doing so, they provided reform leadership on behalf of peoples understood as Hindus, Muslims, and so on.

Therefore, reform built on the communal identities that toleration generated became the political ground on which Indians began to organise themselves as a people.[28]

The communal fault lines along which social reform was organised were only further strengthened when nationalists carried forward their reform agenda when exercising power under British constitutional statutes in the first half of the twentieth century. These constitutional statutes, discussed in more detail in Chapters 3 and 4, permitted limited Indian participation in colonial legislatures and government. More importantly, governmental power allowed Indian elites to carry their moral authority into government and to assert sovereign control over the reorganisation of Indian society.[29]

Thus, reform made far-reaching changes in religious traditions as envisaged by the sovereign imagination of emerging nationalist elites. Nonetheless, the authority to reform and remake religious practice was by and large asserted along the lines of religious community. For example, temple-entry legislation did not seek to open religious spaces to all persons but to all classes and sections of Hindus; animal sacrifice was not banned, for instance, as an act of cruelty but as a deficiency or atavistic feature in the Hindu community; similarly *devadasi* reform was articulated not in terms of generalised coercion but as the reform of a deviant Hinduism that exploited women.[30] Similar examples can also be drawn from Muslim law reform at least up to the Shariat Act of 1937, which will be drawn out in greater detail in Chapter 2. However, since the passing of the Shariat Act in 1937 law makers have not taken on the burden of Muslim reform, a problem they shied away from even after Indian independence, primarily on grounds that they did not have the legitimacy to press reform on a minority beleaguered by the partition of British India.[31]

Running up to Indian independence, this model of toleration and reform, and of the Indian people from which it drew succour, came under strain as the Indian Constitution aspired to ground its conception of the Indian people in individual citizenship. The development of this conceptualisation of citizenship and of the people on which it draws upon will be discussed in greater detail in Chapters 3 and 4. For the present discussion it is sufficient to note that religious freedom in the Indian Constitution was, as elaborated earlier in this chapter, granted to individuals and to religious denominations. In addition, the state was granted the power to reform religious practice. However, both denominational freedom and state power to reform denominational practice were understood as having to be made consistent with individual citizenship. In fact, the *Shirur Mutt* case is a good example of adjudicatory practice drawing a balance between denominational rights, the state's power to reform and regulate religion and the overall constitutional scheme founded in individual citizenship. In this scheme, denominational rights were interpreted as clearly subject to the secular and sovereign power of the state to reform and regulate religion on behalf of all citizens.

Similarly, at the time of the framing of the constitution, the personal law system also came under similar pressure to be reconciled with a constitutional imagination founded on individual citizenship, a challenge resolved by the act of deferral detailed in Article 44. That is, the provision implicitly authorised and carried over the personal law framework into the Indian Constitution but nonetheless directed the state to work towards a uniform civil code applicable to all citizens. Personal laws and their possible contributions to a communal constitutional imagination will be discussed in greater detail in Chapter 2. However, even as the Constitution was broadly disposed towards individual citizenship, it did leave open space for prior colonial forms of religious identification associated with toleration and reform. It is in this gap between colonial and contemporary forms of governing religion that the reformist court of Gajendragadkar stepped in to upend the *Shirur Mutt* approach to essential religious practices and reinforce an earlier colonial and communal form of identifying religion and religious practice. Consequently, it is by foregrounding the continued presence of this conceptualisation of religion that this chapter elaborates its argument about the communal character of Indian constitutional identity.

Essential Religion as a Call to Politics

As already highlighted, much of the legal scholarship approaches the essential practices test developed by the Gajendragadkar court solely as a problem about constitutional interpretation. Against this manner of evaluating the essential practices test, this chapter has attempted to shift the ground of constitutional understanding from contested norms to a contest about the character of the people for whom the right to religion must be defended. That is, it has presented the hypothesis that identifying religion through its essential truths is also a conceptual frame that holds together ideas about India, its people, and the problem of establishing government for its diverse peoples.

Of course, the right to religion that the Constitution grants to groups is specifically vested in 'denominations' which constitutional practice has understood narrowly for the most part. However, the wide discretion that the Gajendragadkar Supreme Court permitted to determine essential religious practices has allowed subsequent courts delimiting religious freedom to draw on colonial toleration to cast denominational rights broadly. That is, drawing on aspects of the colonial regulation of religion, the contemporary court has on occasion cast or delimited denominations as identical or nearly identical with the Indian people themselves. Through one such instance where the essential religion has been defined in very broad terms, the following section illustrates the way the essential practices test is deployed to communally inflect Indian constitutional identity.

The *Ram Janmabhoomi–Babri Masjid* Case

The *Ram Janmabhoomi–Babri Masjid* case (hereafter the *Ayodhya* case), which the Supreme Court brought to an uneasy close in 2019, represents one of the most polarising moments that besieged the constitutional politics of contemporary India. Recounting the progress of the case across colonial and postcolonial India, this section demonstrates the way the case framed religion through the prism of essential practices, and, in turn, the way religion framed by essential practices was institutionally mobilised to identify the Indian people in sharply communal terms.

The *Ayodhya* case decided conflicting claims to a religious structure variously called the Ram Janmabhoomi or Babri Masjid located in the north Indian town of Ayodhya and is a dispute older than the Indian republic itself. At its core the case pertains to a property dispute between various Hindu and Muslim groups over a sixteenth-century temple–mosque complex.

On the one hand, the Hindu parties asserted their rights to the disputed property on the grounds of its association with the birthplace of the religio-cultural and mythological hero Rama. The Muslim parties, on the other hand, claimed that the structure was built as a mosque by Babur, the first of the Moghul emperors, and that its ownership should vest with those charged with its management. The passions raised by the dispute spiralled out of control in 1991 when the temple–mosque structure was demolished by a Hindu mob. Drawing on this fraught dispute, this section sketches the form in which communal religious groups understood as bearers of essential truths have transformed a local dispute into a fissure defining the Indian people.

The *Ayodhya* Case in Colonial Courts

As it first presented itself in court in 1885, the Ayodhya dispute pertained to the shared use of a religious and cultural space that was judicially framed as a property dispute. Thus, claiming ownership over a religious structure called the Ram Chabutra (an open-air platform and Hindu shrine within the premises of the disputed property), the *mahant*, or priest, at the *chabutra* petitioned the sub-judge of the trial court at Faizabad for permission to build a permanent structure over the *chabutra*. However, the *mutawalli*, or caretaker, of the mosque at the property contested the *mahant's* claims, contending that as owners they had granted Hindu devotees permission to use the property and that this was not to be construed as the right of ownership or possession.

The trial court found that the *chabutra* was in the possession of Hindus, who performed their traditional rites at the structure. However, it observed that

> [t]his place is not like other places where the owner has got the right to construct any building as he likes ... The place where the Hindus worship is in their possession from of old and their ownership cannot be questioned and around it there is the wall of the mosque and the word Allah is inscribed on it ... and if permission is given to Hindus for constructing a temple then ... thousands of people will be killed. For this reason of breach of law and order the officers have restrained the parties from making any new construction. So this court also considers it to be proper that *awarding permission to construct the temple at this juncture is to lay the foundation of riot and murder ... between Hindus and Muslims.*[32] (Emphasis added)

Scholarship shows that there was legitimate nervousness on the part of the colonial administration to permit the contending parties to carry on their practices in such proximity to each other as there were known instances of past violence.[33] However, if the *mahant* and his community were adjudged owners, it is baffling that the court permitted the state to abdicate its responsibility to protect the enjoyment of property that logically follows ownership. Further, the assessment that communities that have lived with each other for generations were destined to 'riot and murder' also seems an extreme interpretation of the problem and to fly in the face of the facts. However, appellate judges only seemed to reinforce such puzzling assessments about the nature of the problem.

Thus, the district judge rephrased the lower court judgment and stated that in the circumstances of the case it was redundant to assert that the 'ownership and possession' of the *chabutra* was with Hindus. However, he found that there was evidence to suggest that one portion of the temple–mosque complex was used by Muslims and that the Ram Chabutra was occupied by Hindus. Significantly, he also described the property as representing the divisions between Hindus and Muslims, especially the historical injustice committed by a Muslim emperor on his Hindu subjects. As he noted, *[i]t is most unfortunate that a masjid should have been built on land specially held sacred by the Hindus,* but as that event occurred 356 years ago it is too late now to remedy the grievance. All that can be done is to maintain the parties in status quo.[34] (Emphasis added)

This is a more explicit statement of the problem that the disputed structure was understood to have posed, and one that replays the political sociology upon which toleration was built. That is, India was cast as a land of divided people, of whom the division between Hindus and their erstwhile Muslim rulers was particularly significant. Thrust into government, it was the obligation of the British as rulers to protect religious liberty and neutrally hold the peace among this uneasy mix of peoples. Of course this was only how the British viewed their role as rulers. However, ideas are not without consequence as the British conception of their Indian subjects played a significant role in shaping the contending positions in the case as emblematic of the Indian body politic – a position restated as the case was sent on further appeal.

In the court of second appeal, it was held that the disputed property was in the joint use of both Hindus and Muslims but that there was insufficient evidence to support the proprietary claims of the Hindus. However, as in the lower court, the appeal court also cast the disputed structure as a mark of historic injustice suffered by Hindus at the hands of Muslim rulers. Thus Justice W. Young, Judicial Commissioner, Oudh, observed that

this spot is situated within the precinct of the grounds surrounding a mosque erected some 350 years ago *owing to the bigotry and tyranny of the Emperor Babur,* who purposely chose this holy spot according to Hindu legend as the site of his mosque.[35] (Emphasis added)

These excerpted extracts from the *Ayodhya* case as it moved through the colonial courts illustrate the way colonial judges cast an ordinary property dispute into a conflict pertaining to the Indian people understood as divided between 'Hindus' and 'Muslims'. Historical research suggests that claims regarding the sacred geography of Hindus as a people or the tyranny of Islamic rule were not led as evidence at trial.[36] Further, socio-cultural evidence has suggested that social life at Ayodhya was deeply intertwined, and even though there were significant instances of conflicts regarding various parts of the disputed structure, they were not beyond the reach of recorded instances of reconciliation and resolution. However, colonial characterisation of the disputed structure cast it as nothing but an emblem of a people divided as Hindus and Muslims, which, in turn, was also replayed in the way colonial courts organised the dispute.[37] Thus, by characterising the dispute in this fashion, the court transformed a local property conflict into a national dispute pertaining to the body politic or the Indian people as a whole. It was this transformed dispute that was passed on to the republic of independent India.

The Contours of the Contemporary Dispute

The decree of the colonial courts held until December 1949 when, at the cusp of the transition to independent India, miscreants broke into the disputed property and installed idols under the central dome of the Mosque at the disputed structure. The forceful installation of the idols resulted in the provincial government attaching the property, permitting limited worship of idols installed at the site and placing the property in the possession of a receiver until disputes raised by the installation of idols were judicially settled. This attachment gave rise to a set of civil suits which were the basis of the present *Ayodhya* case.

Of the five suits filed in the case, one was withdrawn and the other four divided into three sets of claims for title and possession of the disputed property. The Muslim parties claimed that the disputed structure was a mosque constructed by the Moghul emperor Babur upon either barren land or, in the alternative, on the ruins of a temple. As it had been dedicated to the community, they claimed that they were in possession of the property until 1949, when they were dispossessed. However, they also admitted the existence of a *chabutra* in the outer courtyard at which Hindus were permitted to pray. On the other hand, the 'Hindu' parties made two kinds of claims. First, the 'Nirmohi Akhara', a religious sect that managed the *chabutra* and other religious structures outside the mosque, claimed that the disputed structure was never a mosque. Therefore, as the group traditionally associated with the management of the structure, the Akhara argued that they should be given possession of the entire premises. Second, other groups contended that even if the attached disputed property was a mosque, it ceased to be so when it was substantially damaged in a communal riot in the year 1934. All Hindu parties claim that after this date the property was not used as a mosque by Muslim parties and that they were in possession of the property, which they believe to be the birthplace of Rama.

While these suits were pending, the attachment order was modified in 1986 to open the locks of the disputed property and permit all members of the public to offer respects to the idols forcibly installed at the disputed structure. This was a significant alteration of the status quo, which until this point only allowed the performance of rituals at the site in a restricted manner by specially appointed priests. The alteration of the earlier attachment order is attributed to the machinations of the then ruling Congress party pandering to the demands of electoral politics, especially to what they believed to be Hindu interests. This, in turn, decisively catapulted the problem of the disputed structure onto the stage of national politics and set off a chain of events that eventually led to the demolition of the mosque at the disputed site in 1992.

The demolition unleashed a wave of violence across the country, prompting the central government to enact the Acquisition of Certain Areas at Ayodhya Act, 1993. This statute acquired the disputed property and abated all pending suits regarding the property. Separately the government initiated a presidential reference to the Supreme Court, asking the question '(w)hether a Hindu temple or any Hindu religious structure existed prior to the construction of the *Ram Janma Bhumi–Babri Masjid* ... in the area on which the structure stood'. The Supreme Court refused to answer the presidential reference, struck down the provisions of the statute that abated all pending suits, and directed the central government to hold the disputed property as a receiver until the earlier suits, now reinstated, were decided.[38] Accordingly, the Allahabad High Court delivered its decision in the revived suits of the *Ayodhya* case in September 2010[39] and, on appeal, the Supreme Court finally disposed of the matter in 2019.[40]

Of these sprawling judgments that run over several thousand pages, the present comment only emphasises the way the courts continued to present this dispute as a national problem produced by a polity divided by religious interests.[41] As a property dispute, the courts could clearly have avoided approaching this dispute as one animated by irreconcilable religious sentiment. That is, the courts could have delimited the dispute to title and possession or the fact that the matter had been conclusively litigated and resolved in colonial courts. Instead, the courts of independent India allowed themselves to be drawn into a whole set of ancillary questions that included, among others: (1) Was the disputed structure the birthplace of Rama? (2) Was the disputed structure a mosque? (3) Did a temple exist at the disputed site where the mosque currently stands and was the temple demolished to build the mosque? (3) Did the emperor Babar build a mosque at the site? (4) Was there continuous worship of the contending communities at the disputed site?[42] These questions pushed the case away from questions of property rights and the legal rules barring reopening of settled legal disputes, and invited claimants to demonstrate that the disputed property was an essential aspect of their divided religious traditions. In doing so, parties were permitted to float free of the specific spatial contours of the dispute and characterise their claims on behalf of a national community of Hindu or Muslim people. It is this dimension of the High Court and Supreme Court decisions that must now be surveyed to demonstrate the form in which the courts modelled a communal people at odds with each other.

Parochialising Rama, Communalising the Nation

Of the Supreme Court and High Court decisions, the Supreme Court made a marked attempt to steer its decision away from the essential religious truths of the contending communities in the *Ram Janmabhoomi* dispute. Even so, both decisions are dependent on characterising the disputed property as divided by the essential truths of contending religious communities and whose divisions also constitute a central fissure in the Indian body politic or its people.

In the High Court this commitment to essential religious practice is most pronounced where two of the three judges were explicitly committed to asserting that the disputed property embodied the essential truths of the Hindu community. Deciding in this fashion was not straightforward as the dispute was produced by breaking into and vandalising a property in the management of another religious tradition. Nonetheless, the unsatisfactory answer they provide is rooted in the antiquity of Hindu claims and their unjust displacement by Islamic conquest. In the case of Justice Sharma, this went as far as stretching historical facts to assert that the disputed property was the precise site where Rama was born. That is, he presents local beliefs and accounts of travellers, gazetteers and anthropological records on local beliefs as indisputable evidence that Rama was born at the disputed site. As a heroic figure from mythic time no such claim about Rama can be satisfactorily justified, but the object of Justice Sharma's efforts is clear enough – the site must be presented as an object of Hindu veneration from a time that preceded the establishment of the mosque.[43]

Judge Sharma's reference to history and to the belief of devotees reveals considerable confusion whether Rama is a sacred figure located in historical time or whether he is a deified but mythological hero believed to have been born at the disputed site. This confusion is put to rest in some measure by Judge Agarwal, who casts the issue in terms of popular religious sentiment, an issue he posed by asking whether the disputed property was the birthplace of Rama according to the tradition, belief and faith of Hindus.[44] He answered the question in the affirmative by asserting that Hindu belief and practice had come to converge on the disputed property to establish that Hindus believed the site to be of essential significance to their faith. In turn, judicially divined popular belief became one among other qualifying reasons granting Hindu parties a proprietary right to a part of the disputed property.

To both these judges, the centrality of Rama to the Hindu religion was woven into evidence that they believed supported the fact that the mosque at the disputed property was built over a demolished Hindu temple. This finding allowed the judges to pull together a Hindu people who were tied to the disputed property even prior to the construction of the mosque. By extension, the Hindus are also imagined as a political community pulled together by the common historical wrongs suffered at the hands of alien Muslim rule.

Claiming rights to the mosque that they controlled for many hundred years, the Muslim parties could also assert that their mosque was an essential aspect of their tradition. However, even as they claimed that the mosque was dedicated for the benefit of the community, and that defending their claims to the mosque constituted an essential part of their religious tradition, the High Court set aside their contention relying on an earlier ruling in the earlier Supreme Court decision in *Ismail Faruqui v. Union of India*.[45] In this case, the Supreme Court had held that the Muslim community would have to demonstrate that a mosque had a special place in the Islamic tradition for it to be adjudged essential to the Islamic faith.[46] This demand is a clearly asymmetric demand that Muslims would have to discharge, but bracketing such normative aspects of this judgment, it is important to note that the local Muslims, like the Hindus, were now no longer disputing a local religious structure that was disputed and yet concurrently used by these communities for a considerable period of time. On the contrary, Hindu and Muslim identities were pulled together as embodiments of axiomatically and doctrinally organised divisions that constituted the Indian people. Consequently, this conceptualisation of a people divided by their religious truths formed a central aspect of the court's decision that divided the property into three parts between the three main claimants to the property.

On appeal the Supreme Court made a significant effort to distance itself from explicit reference to the essential religious beliefs of either the Hindus or the Muslims. After satisfying itself of the *bona fide* assertion of property rights claims by the contending parties, the court's efforts were directed at resolving what it saw to be the knotted issues of ownership and possession of the disputed property. These issues were considered alongside preliminary objections, important among which were the contentions that the suits were barred by time and that the doctrine of *res judicata* prevented the court from reopening substantially similar issues that were previously adjudicated. Having held that the claims of the parties were not time barred and that *res judicata* did not apply to the dispute, the court proceeded to consider the issues of title, possession, as well as the acts of aggression that had marked the recent history to control the disputed property.

As with the High Court decision, the present discussion does not undertake a full technical appraisal of the court's reasons except to note that the court resolved the problem of title and possession by holding that both Hindu and Muslim parties had demonstrated possession of different parts of the property, that the idols were illegally placed in the disputed structure in 1949 and that the demolition of the disputed structure in 1991 was an illegal act. This determination of ownership and possession was arrived at without any significant reference to the essential truths of the Hindu and Muslim religions. Even so, when fashioning its final relief, the court decreed the disputed property entirely in favour of the Hindu parties. However, having also found that Muslim parties had demonstrated possession of the mosque before it was demolished, the court ordered the government to make alternative land available to the Muslim parties.[47] This is a curious aspect of the court's reasoning and requires closer examination.

The Supreme Court justified its decision to shift Muslims from the disputed site on multiple grounds. Procedurally, the court took the view that the earlier High Court decision that partitioned the suit property among the three main litigants was not asserted in the pleadings. Significantly, the relief that the Supreme Court granted the Muslim parties was also not drawn from the pleadings of the respective parties but from the extraordinary power granted to the court by Article 142 to do complete justice in matters pending before the court. Substantively, the court granted the Hindu parties complete possession over the whole of the property on the grounds that their claims to possession stood on a stronger footing. The legal correctness of the Supreme Court's reading of the relief granted by the High Court and its finding that the Hindus' claims were better supported by evidence are technical questions that will be bracketed from the present discussion.[48] However, against the background of the argument in this chapter it is relevant to highlight an incidental observation by the Supreme Court that it chose not to divide the property between the disputing parties as it was not in 'the interest of either of the parties or secure a lasting sense of peace and security'.

Though the court has made considerable effort to keep away all references to casting the disputed property as a contest between communities divided by their essential truths, this last comment bears a striking resemblance to colonial courts that saw the dispute as generated by an irreconcilably divided body politic. Further, though the Supreme Court carefully avoided framing the dispute like colonial courts in the main portion of its judgment, this colonial perspective is slipped into an unusual addendum that formed part of the judgment.[49] In this addendum the Supreme Court slides straight back into casting the dispute as one requiring the resolution of the question whether 'the disputed structure is the holy birthplace of Lord Ram as per the faith trust and belief of Hindus'[50] Consequently, drawing on scriptural and historical sources as well as oral testimony, the dispute is cast as a problem involving the essential doctrinal faith of the Hindu religion. Unlike in the High Court, the addendum does not make a pretence of having to balance this essential truth of the Hindus with a similar claim that could be made by Muslim parties. Thus, it is alongside this slanted deployment of essential Hindu truth in the addendum that the Supreme Court has put a lid on this long-standing dispute.

It is unclear whether the addendum to the judgment will be held by a future court to be legally binding. However, by fastening the disputed property to the essential doctrinal truths of the Hindu religion, the addendum has continued a long tradition of state practice that identifies religion and religious freedom with the truths of a people. Of course, the addendum is at best only a footnote to the *Ayodhya* judgment, but its presence in the judgment demonstrates the influence that the communal imagination of the essential practices test continues to exert on Indian state practice.

The *Ayodhya* case is a stark example of the way the essential practices formulation has communally inflected Indian constitutional identity. As already noted, the communal identification of the Indian people is not a necessary consequence that must follow either from the design of Articles 25 and 26 of the Constitution or even from the essential practices test as it was crafted before the Gajendragadkar Supreme Court. However, the wide judicial discretion to fashion essential doctrines permitted by the Gajendragadkar Supreme Court has skewed the determination of religious freedom towards the communal conceptualisation of the Indian people.[51] Consequently, it is along the range of possibilities in the interpretation of religious freedom that the *Ayodhya* case stands out as a particularly stark example of the communal as well as polarising effects of the essential practices approach to delimiting religion.

Constitutional design and practice, as already noted, point to the possibility of alternative normative choices that interpret religious freedom and consequently also conceptualise the Indian people differently. That is, it is possible to fashion religious freedom in ways that push aside the communal sensibilities that the essential practices test foregrounds and cast religious freedom in ways consistent with the people understood as a community of individual citizens. Consequently, drawing on these alternative normative possibilities, this chapter draws to a close by locating the scheme of the essential practices test against other normative choices and their related forms of modelling the Indian people.

The Communal State and Its Alternatives

The efforts to describe and identify the communal tendencies that have shaped Indian constitutional practice, in both this chapter and this entire book, are set against the Constitution's broader liberal aspirations. These goals and normative frames consistent with them were mentioned briefly when referring to scholarship that interrogated the essential practices test on grounds that it sits uneasily with the normative scheme of the Constitution and its secular values. However, this liberal and secular dimension of the Indian Constitution was bracketed to explain and detail the essential practices test as an important strand in Indian constitutional reasoning. Having done so, it is now important to juxtapose these normative choices that the Constitution offers against the communal obstacle that this chapter has detailed. This task is illustrated through a brief examination of another recent Supreme Court decision as it has laid out normative choices available to bypass the communally inflected approach to delimiting religious freedom.

The *Sabarimala* Decision

In *Indian Young Lawyers Association v. State of Kerala*,[52] the Supreme Court considered a constitutional challenge to a customary practice that barred women between the ages of ten and fifty access to the well-known Ayyappan temple at Sabarimala in Kerala. The temple was under the overall superintendence of temple administration organised by the Kerala government and was subject to temple-entry legislation in Kerala that required all Hindu temples of a public character to permit access to all sections and classes of Hindus. According to denominational practice, this temple permitted access to all persons both Hindu and non-Hindu. Nonetheless, custom barred women in their menstruating years from accessing the temple on grounds that this was against the wishes of the deity at Sabarimala. Besides being defended as part of the religious freedom of the Ayyappans at Sabarimala, this practice was also said to be authorised by rules under the temple statute that permitted customary exclusion of women. Challenging this practice and the rules that were said to authorise it, the appellants argued that a temple, especially one under government superintendence, could not oversee practices that undermined existing law on temple entry and broader constitutional values.

This case generated much public debate on the extent to which the state ought to intervene in religious issues. However, glossing over the uproar that the case produced as well as the finer legal detail that was put up for resolution, this section only spotlights the way the judgment approached temple exclusion as an essential aspect of the Ayyappan tradition.

Through four separate decisions rendered in its *Sabarimala* judgment, the Supreme Court pronounced that the custom of excluding women at Sabarimala was illegal and unconstitutional. However, it is not this outcome that secured temple entry for women, but the extent to which the court was able to free itself from seeking out axiomatically organised essential religious truths or doctrines that this discussion will emphasise. Of course, not all the decisions in the judgment cut loose from their attachment to the essential practices framework. Thus, of the plurality of decisions that made up the majority decision to ban the exclusion of women from the temple, the joint decision of Justices Misra and Khanwilkar completely relied on the essential practices test. Their argument proceeds on the assumption that all Hindu women have a right to religious freedom guaranteed under Article 25(1). Consequently, as the Ayyappans as a denomination had not shown sufficient evidence to establish that the exclusion of Hindu women was an essential truth of their religious tradition, they could not displace the right of Hindu women to exercise their fundamental rights to practise their religion.[53] Nonetheless, it is important to note that this line of reasoning brought different approaches to essential religious practice to a head – that of the female devotees of Lord Ayyappan to freely practice religion and that of the Ayyapans as a denomination to access their religious traditions and exclude women from the shrine at Sabarimala.

Unlike Misra and Khanwilkar, all the other judges moved away in different degrees from the determining influence of the essential practices. The essential practices argument was only peripherally significant to Justice Nariman, who organised his opinion around the discriminatory potential of the temple exclusion rule issued under the Kerala Places of Worship Act. To this end he first pushed aside any demand to judicially consider the relevance of essential practice related arguments by holding that the Ayyapans were not a denomination whose essential practices required determination or recognition. Having done so, he organised his decision around the equal right of women to observe their religious faith as provided for in Article 25 and, most significantly, the fact that the temple exclusion rule violated

Article 15(1) of the Constitution, which prohibited discrimination based on, among other grounds, sex.[54]

Unlike Nariman, Misra and Khanwilkar, Justices Chandrachud and Malhotra subjected the essential practices test to searching enquiry and critique. Justice Chandrachud's opinion turns on his conception of constitutional morality, which he outlines as a normative orientation in the Constitution, especially in its equality provisions, that sought to transform and redress systemic discrimination against marginalised groups like women and *dalit*s. It is this transformative constitutional vision that helped him settle the claims of women demanding access to the temple as worshipers in their favour and against the conflicting demands of the institutional authorities seeking to defend custom and tradition. Importantly, he deploys constitutional morality to test essential religious practices by arguing that essential practices could be subjected to the anti-discriminatory aspirations of the Indian Constitution. In particular, he draws on the abolition of untouchability in Article 17 to argue that notions of purity and pollution that have powered the exclusionary form of caste society are also impermissibly at work in the exclusion of women from temples accessible to the public. Thus, his conception of religious freedom qualified the search for essential religious truth, subjecting it to secular public standards grounded on the transformative vision of the Indian Constitution, especially its commitment to equality and the abolition of untouchability in all forms.[55] That is, religious freedom is not seen as a stand-alone section of the Constitution but is tied into and read along with the other parts of the Constitution, especially fundamental rights, that emphasise the Constitution's transformative vision.

Like Justices Nariman, Misra and Khanwilkar, Justice Chandrachud also elected to permit the entry of women into the Sabarimala shrine. However, the dissenting decision of Justice Indu Malhotra voted to permit the shrine to hold on to its exclusionary customary practice. This decision also floats free from the essential practices test in a familiar manner that nonetheless bears recounting. In contrast to 'constitutional morality', the normative value that organised Justice Chandrachud's decision, Justice Malhotra's decision is animated by a commitment to toleration and pluralism. That is, she argued that courts ought not to second guess the constitutional rationality of religious practices, except in exceptional cases like Sati or egregious forms of caste oppression and exclusion. The exclusion of women from temples was to her a customary practice essential to the Ayyappan tradition as they viewed it, and unless the practice disclosed extraordinary injustice it ought to be left undisturbed.[56] In this respect her decision represents a pull back to the original *Shirur Mutt* formulation of the essential practices test, before it was altered by Justice Gajendragadkar, where essential religious practices were held to include all aspects of a tradition as it was viewed by its adherents.

Collectively, these decisions represent a spectrum of normative positions that stack up alongside the Gajendragadkar-inspired essential practices test. The present narration only outlines the broad contours of these options and makes no attempt to choose between or argue for any one of them. On the contrary, recounting these options only makes plausible these alternative normative possibilities. However, could these options available in the *Sabarimala* judgment shine light on institutional practice seeking to break the grip of the essential practices test? This chapter concludes by briefly touching on this question and tying it to the account of the chapters that follow.

Conclusion

Much of this chapter sought to explain the essential practices test as it is nestled within the normative scheme of the Indian Constitution. Even as the test was traced to the colonial state, this chapter has also noted that the essential practices test sits uneasily within the normative structure of the Indian Constitution. However, having illustrated both the historical salience of the essential practices approach and its troubled place in the contemporary Constitution, it could be argued that reasoning like either judges Chandrachud or Malhotra could edge out the communal imprint of the essential practices test.

This is undoubtedly a real possibility. However, as the subsequent chapters will show, delimiting religion or a religious community by searching for its axiomatically organised foundational truths is not just a doctrinal and adjudicatory form of identifying the scope of religious freedom. More importantly, it is an axis along which the Indian people have been modelled. As a form of imagining the Indian people, the search and identification of axiomatically organised essential truth is also echoed in other key aspects of the Constitution. Accordingly, the chapters that follow identify and elaborate the ways axiomatically organised essential religious truth have identified the Indian people and has been woven into the regulation of personal law, minority rights and caste. These schemes of constitutional government interlock with each other to reinforce a communal conception of the Indian people posing a formidable alternative to the Constitution's liberal vision of individual citizenship. It is this alternative conceptualisation of the Indian people as it is nestled in the Indian Constitution that will be examined and elaborated in the chapters that follow.

Notes

1. For example, see Pratap Bhanu Mehta, 'On the Possibility of Religious Pluralism', in *Religious Pluralism, Globalization, and World Politics*, ed. Thomas Banchoff, 71–72 (New York: Oxford University Press, 2008). See also Winnifred Fallers Sullivan, *The Impossibility of Religious Freedom* (Princeton: Princeton University Press, 2007).

2. *Venkataramana Devaru v. State of Mysore* 1958 AIR 255.

3. This is illustrated in the contrasting opinions of Judges Nariman Chandrachud and Malhotra in *Indian Young Lawyers Association v. State of Kerala* MANU/SC/1094/2018; see also Gautam Bhatia, 'Freedom from Community: Individual Rights, Group Life, State Authority and Religious Freedom under the Indian Constitution', *Global Constitutionalism* 5, no. 3 (2016): 351.

4. This author has previously addressed issues arising out of this doctrine in Mathew John, 'Framing Religion in Constitutional Politics: A View from Indian Constitutional Law', *South Asian History and Culture* 10, no. 2 (2019): 124–35; Mathew John, 'Parochialism in Indian Constitutional Reasoning: The Case of Religious Freedom', *Verfassung und Recht in Übersee / Law and Politics in Africa, Asia and Latin America* 51, no. 3 (2018): 332–51.

5. *The Commissioner Hindu Religious Endowments, Madras v. Sri Laxmindra Thirtha Swamiar of Shirur Mutt* MANU/SC/0136/1954 (henceforth *Shirur Mutt*).

6. *Shirur Mutt*, para. 20.

7. *Venkataramana Devaru v. State of Mysore* 1958 AIR 255.

8. *Sastri Yagnapurushadji v. Muldas Bhudardas Vaishya* MANU/SC/0040/1966; *Durgah Committee; Ajmer and Anr. v. Syed Hussain Ali and Ors.* MANU/SC/0063/1961; *Tilkayat Tilkayat Shri Govindlalji Maharaj v. State of Rajastan* MANU/SC/0028/1963.

9. Bhatia, 'Freedom from Community'.

10. *M. H. Qureshi v. State of Bihar* MANU/SC/0027/1958.

11. *Ismail Faruqui v. UOI* MANU/SC/0860/1994.

12. *Tilkayat Tilkayat Shri Govindlalji Maharaj v. State of Rajastan* MANU/SC/0028/1963.

13. *Jagdishwaranand v. Police Commissioner, Calcutta* MANU/SC/0050/1983.

14. *S. P. Mittal v. Union of India* AIR MANU/SC/0532/1982.

15. *Nikhil Soni v. Union of India* MANU/RH/1345/2015.

16. For example, see Bhatia, 'Freedom from Community'; Anup Surendranath, 'Essential Practices Doctrine: Towards Inevitable Constitutional Burial' *Journal of the National Human Rights Commission, India* 15 (2016): 159; Ronojoy Sen, *Articles of Faith: Religion, Secularism and Indian Supreme Court* (New Delhi: Oxford University Press, 2010).

17. For example, see opinion of Judge Chandrachud in *Indian Young Lawyers Association v. State of Kerala* MANU/SC/1094/2018.

18. For example, see Rawls, *Political Liberalism*; Jakob De Roover, *Europe, India, and the Limits of Secularism* (New Delhi: Oxford University Press, 2015).

19. See Smith, *India as a Secular State*; Chatterjee, 'Secularism and Tolerance'; De Roover and Balagangadhara, 'Liberty Tyranny and the Will of God'.

20. For example, see Mani, 'Contentious Traditions'; Bernard S. Cohn, *Colonialism and Its Forms of Knowledge: The British in India* (Princeton: Princeton University Press, 1996); Nicholas B. Dirks, *Castes of Mind: Colonialism and the Making of Modern India* (New Delhi: Permanent Black, 2003).

21. Art. XXIII, Judicial Plan of 1772, IOR/H/420, 1772 (Extended by Justice Elijah Impey in 1882 to include 'Inheritance and succession as also to include the provision that cases where no specific directions had been given the courts was to act according to Justice, equity and good conscience'. ss. LX and XCIII Regulation VI 1781).

22. This has been done elsewhere. For example, see Smith, *India as a Secular State*.

23. See discussion in Mani, 'Contentious Traditions'.

24. See Mani, 'Contentious Traditions'; Andrea Major, *Pious Flames: European Encounters with Sati 1500–1830* (New Delhi: Oxford University Press, 2006); De Roover and Balagangadhara, 'Liberty Tyranny and the Will of God'.

25. See Also Chandra Mallampalli, *Race, Religion and Law in Colonial India: Trials of an Interracial Family* (Cambridge, UK: Cambridge University Press, 2011); Teena Purohit, *The Aga Khan Case: Religion and Identity in Colonial India* (Sew edn, Cambridge, MA: Harvard University Press, 2012).

26. Mani, 'Contentious Traditions'.

27. Mani, 'Contentious Traditions'.

28. Chatterjee, *The Nation and Its Fragments*.

29. Chatterjee, *The Nation and Its Fragments*.

30. Chatterjee, 'Secularism and Tolerance'.

31. Chatterjee, 'Secularism and Tolerance'.

32. Abdul Gafoor Noorani, *The Babri Masjid Question, 1528–2003: 'A Matter of National Honour'*, vol. 1 (New Delhi: Tulika Books, 2004) 181.

33. Noorani, *The Babri Masjid Question*.

34. Noorani, *The Babri Masjid Question*, 1: 182–84.

35. Noorani, *The Babri Masjid Question*, 1:186–88.

36. Geetanjali Srikantan, 'Reexamining Secularism' *Journal of Law, Religion and State* 5, no. 2 (2017): 117.

37. Sushil Srivastava, 'How the British Saw the Issue', in *Anatomy of a Confrontation: The Babri Masjid–Ramjanmabhumi Issue*, ed. Sarvepalli Gopal, 38–57 (New Delhi; New York, NY Penguin Books, 1991). See also Ashis Nandy, Shikha Trivedy, Shail Mayaram and Achyut Yagnik, *Creating a Nationality: The Ramjanmabhumi Movement and Fear of the Self* (New Delhi: Oxford University Press, USA 1998).

38. *Ismail Faruqui v. Union of India* MANU/SC/0126/1995.

39. *Gopal Singh Visharad and Others v. Zahoor Ahmad and Others* MANU/UP/1185/2010.

40. *M Siddiq v. Mahant Suresh Das* MANU/SC/1538/2019.

41. For a short and useful summary of the High Court decision, see Aparna Chandra, 'Gopal Singh Visharad and Ors V. Zahoor Ahmad and Ors., O.S.Nos. 1/1989, 3/1989, 4/1989, 5/1989: A Summary of the Babri Masjid-Ram Janm Bhoomi Decision', 2010, SSRN eLibrary, http://papers.ssrn.com/sol3/papers.cfm?abstract_id=1690803, accessed 17 February 2011.

42. See also Chandra, 'Gopal Singh Visharad and Ors V. Zahoor Ahmad and Ors.'

43. Judge Sharma, MANU/SC/0126/1995 Vol. 4.

44. Judge Agarwal, MANU/SC/0126/1995, paras 4079–4418.

45. MANU/SC/0126/1995.

46. In addition Justice Sharma also held that the mosque itself was not constructed according to the tenets of Islam for the following reasons: (1) The mosque did not have minarets as mandated by Islamic tenets. (2) It was unusual and against Islamic tenets for a mosque to be surrounded by graveyards. (3) It was unusual for a mosque to be surrounded by Hindu religious structures. (4) The mosque did not have a bathing pool for devotees to wash themselves before worship. (5) There were images and idols on the walls of the disputed property. (6) Discussing the nature of Islamic public trusts or *wakfs* he said the property on which a mosque is constructed must belong to the person dedicating the *wakf* if such dedication was to be valid. As an invader he held that Babur could not have owned the disputed property and therefore the mosque was not validly constructed according to the tenets of Islam. (7) Lastly, and strangely, Justice Sharma even seems to hold that the demolition itself was a reason to assert that no mosque existed at the place and that no Islamic religious rites are followed at the site as a result. See Chandra, 'Gopal Singh Visharad and Ors V. Zahoor Ahmad and Ors.'

47. *M Siddiq v. Mahant Suresh Das*, paras 768–805.

48. *M Siddiq v. Mahant Suresh Das*, paras 768–805..

49. *M Siddiq v. Mahant Suresh Das.*

50. Addendum to *M Siddiq v. Mahant Suresh Das* MANU/SC/1538/2019, para 31.

51. This is well described by Ronojoy Sen who points out that essential practices have tended to delimit localised denominational practices in the image of Hindu high traditions, where the Hindu religion often stands in for a Hindu people. Sen, *Articles of Faith.*

52. MANU/SC/1094/2018

53. *Indian Young Lawyers Association v. State of Kerala*, paras 122–23

54. *Indian Young Lawyers Association v. State of Kerala*, paras 174–77

55. *Indian Young Lawyers Association v. State of Kerala*, paras 258, 286.

56. *Indian Young Lawyers Association v. State of Kerala*, para 304.

2

The Communal Image of the People in India's Personal Laws

This chapter pulls together an account of personal laws across colonial and contemporary India to illustrate the manner in which the identity of the Indian people is constitutionally cast in communal terms. Personal laws, as they developed in colonial India, have clearly been carried over into the legal scheme of contemporary India. However, personal laws were designed to be a receding part of the Constitution of independent India. Article 44 is a directive principle that obliged the Indian state to work towards a uniform civil code, presumably by doing away with personal laws. Even so, decades after the adoption of the Constitution, the inability to secure a uniform civil code has produced much discussion, either pronouncing failure of this normative objective[1] or justifying the continuation of personal laws as consistent with the Indian constitutional order.[2] Bracketing a full-blooded consideration of these normative points of view, this chapter draws on these alternative positions to disclose and make apparent contrasting forms of identifying the Indian people.

Of the various ways in which the Indian people are identified in discussions on personal law, this chapter demonstrates the overlapping salience of a communally inflected conception of the Indian people as foregrounded in Chapter 1. That is, extending the discussion on colonial toleration, this chapter demonstrates constitutional organisation and practice of personal law that actively draws on and entrenches the very same religiously organised and communal vision of the Indian people.

The Background: Peoples and Their Laws

The historical roots that bind personal laws to contemporary Indian law have been previously traced to colonial toleration. The commitment to tolerate constituted personal laws as objects of forbearance but through a peculiar legal reconstruction and reduction of local religious and cultural practices. This reduction of religious traditions to axiomatically applicable propositions identified as essential doctrines was outlined in Chapter 1. Additionally, a complement to this form of toleration was the manner in which personal laws were crafted as a self-conscious act of legal recovery that must now be briefly recounted.

Thus, drawing on the expertise of antiquarians, linguists, historians and Indologists, the toleration of personal laws was tied to its recovery and re-constitution by the East Indian Company after it took over the administration of Bengal following the Battle of Plassey in 1757. The colonial approach to personal law identified them as the norms of antiquity that had previously bound the Indian people but had over time largely lost its pan-Indian influence and authority. Consequently, having committed to rule by toleration and forbearance, the colonial state assumed the duty to recover these laws so that they could be rightfully restored to their subjects understood primarily as 'Hindu' and 'Muslim' people.[3]

Marking Out the Law of a Hindu People

To take the example of Hindu law as it was shaped by this sprawling reconstructive project, the effort to recover Hindu law was centred on the *dharma sastras*, or the religio-legal texts that were believed to apply to the Hindu people. Duncan Derrett describes the way this recovery was made possible by the colonial patronage of sastric learning.[4] In particular, he emphasises the way colonial patronage absorbed the *dharma sastras* as the predictable fixed and axiomatically applicable laws governing family relations of those who came to be known as the Hindu subjects of the British colonial state. However, this was not quite how the dharma sastric tradition applied its rules to those who came under its sway.

The legal tradition embodied by the *dharma sastras* was premised on the belief that it upheld *dharma*, or the eternal laws that maintain right order in the world.[5] The order of *dharma* was sourced from divine revelation, text and custom and was ascertained and maintained by drawing on traditions of well-regarded interpretations of these sources. In addition, the traditional practice of the *dharma sastras* was decidedly not statist, and conformity was not predominantly secured through the threat of legally sanctioned coercion.

That is, the normative rules of the *dharma sastras* depended far less on the centralised authority and recognition by state power than on social acceptance subtly wrung and coaxed by local forms of authority. These local authorities could include villages, castes, guilds and families, in addition to the authority of kings and states. In turn, this meant that there was a range of jurisdictions that administered *dharma*, each drawing on common traditions of interpretation from the *sastras* yet tailoring the *sastras* to their specific local requirements.[6]

This had resulted in a legal system in pre-modern India that Donald Davis describes as a

> variegated grouping of local legal systems that had different rules and procedures of law but that were united by a common jurisprudence or legal theory ... In premodern India, the practical legal systems of any two given Hindu communities may have operated quite differently, but they were both likely to respect the 'spirit' of dharmaśāstra and incorporate it into their legal rules, processes, and institutions.[7]

However, presuming a nationally organised Hindu people, the colonial project of legal recovery was driven by the urge for uniformity, certainty and a suspicion of the malleability of the *dharma sastras*, a suspicion that fundamentally altered the plurality that defined the sastric approach to and resolution of legal problems.[8]

The alterations that the British brought to the *dharma sastra* tradition included (*a*) a narrowing and fixing of the sources and texts from which decisions could be rendered, (*b*) requiring the decisions drawing on the *sastras* be made compatible with the axiomatic and deductive reasoning implicit in the doctrine of *stare decisis*, (*c*) fixing the groups or people to whom the *sastra* would apply, (*d*) fixing the topics from within the span of the *dharma sastras* that would be recognised or tolerated by the colonial state and (*e*) eventually abolishing the *sastris*, or experts who assisted courts, in determining the applicable law in 1864. These changes decisively marked the arrival of a new form of legal regulation in the name of the *dharma sastras* that has since come to be called Anglo-Hindu law.[9]

Anglo-Hindu law has laid considerable emphasis on the doctrine of *stare decisis* and on predictability and certainty in the interpretation of the *dharma sastra* texts. While predictability and certainty are important elements of this new legal form, its establishment was only possible through the transformation of the malleable traditions of interpretation that made up the *dharma sastras*. In turn, the transformation of the *dharma sastras* reworked this tradition into axiomatically applicable doctrines that legally organised the personal relations of the people that Anglo-Hindu law came to call the Hindus.

In practical terms, the emergence of Anglo-Hindu law produced a range of problems. First, the *dharma sastras* were only an interpretative framework that could be bent to the unique needs of different social groups. Second, as a tradition of interpretation that could be adopted by different groups, it was unclear how deeply the *dharma sastras* applied on a pan-India level and especially to tribal and untouchable communities. Relatedly, and third, precisely because it was a tradition of interpretation that could be adapted to a range of situations, it could even apply to peoples who were not understood as Hindu by the boundaries that marked Anglo-Hindu law – for example, Muslims[10] and Christians.[11]

Therefore, it was difficult to isolate an identity or a people to whom the *sastra* applied even as this was precisely how Anglo-Hindu law tolerated, reorganised and mis-recognised the *sastra*s. That is, even though classical accounts of the *dharma sastra*s were an intricate, diverse, and pragmatically organised tradition of interpretation bearing on legal problems, the framework of toleration reorganised and cast the sastric tradition as axiomatic doctrines solely applicable to a people identified as a Hindu.

Perceptive colonial administrators noticed that casting the *dharma sastra*s as the laws of a presumptive Hindu people flew in the face of the traditions they sought to mobilise as personal laws. However, these objections have mostly been minor eddies in the onward march of personal laws as an organising pillar of colonial law and administration. Consequently, to emphasise the way the personal law framework came to stand in as the laws of a people such as the Hindus, it is useful to contour a remarkable challenge posed to the personal law framework by the colonial judge James Henry Nelson. Thus, drawing on Nelson's objections, this section will illustrate the way the personal law framework defended its approach to casting personal laws as embodiments of the religious doctrines of the Indian people.

James Nelson and the Problem of Locality and Custom

As a young and ambitious judge in the Madras judicial service, Nelson sought to distinguish himself through a series of detailed comments on the state of Hindu law as he encountered it in the latter part of the nineteenth century.[12] This examination of Hindu Law, born of his own judicial experience, foregrounded what he called the absurdity and injustice of applying what was styled 'Hindu Law' to the great bulk of the population of the Madras province.[13]

Polemically posed, his problem was 'whether such a thing as Hindu Law ... existed in the world'.[14] Following this question Nelson argued that Anglo-Hindu law was not the positive law that governed the bulk of the Hindu population. To the extent that Anglo-Hindu laws held sway, he argued that they likely only applied to a limited set of Brahmin communities. On the contrary, he argued, what mattered were local customs that determined the applicable law, especially in the Madras province, where the bulk of his experience was drawn from. This account of Anglo-Hindu law carried with it the implication that administering Hindu law to groups of people who had little to do with it reneged on the colonial commitment to govern their subjects according to their respective laws.[15] Consequently, to remedy this breach of trust he advocated the establishment of a commission which would determine the relevant customary laws applicable to various local communities.

Nelson's critique was poorly received by the judicial administration, which in turn sealed his chances of rising to the rank of a judge of the High Court.[16] Nonetheless, his argument forced spirited defences of Anglo-Hindu law from both practitioners and scholars. One prominent critic, Justice L. C. Innes of the Madras High Court, met the cutting edge of Nelson's critique by arguing that colonial courts recognised custom, even when it went against the *sastra*, but only when the existence of a custom could be proved.[17] However, unlike Nelson, Innes was not willing to presume that what mattered most were mere usages and customs as this would, by implication, undo the primacy of the *dharma sastra* rules as the generally applicable law of the Hindu people in matters of family relations.

In foregrounding customary practice, Nelson does not explicitly deny or repudiate the existence of a people called the Hindus. However, his conception of the Hindu was clearly different from that of Innes. To Innes, the Hindu was the identity of a people founded in the *sastra* whose axiomatically organised authority he was obliged to follow on account of both statutory instruction and years of judicial precedent. Within this framework the bulk of the Indian population had

> always been divided into Mahomedans and Hindus ... though many of the customs of the non-Mohamedans who are not part of any of the three twice born classes are distinct ..., such non-Mohamedans have all more or less adopted the Hindu religion and laws, and when bringing their contentions before the Courts have stated their cases ... on the assumption that they form part of the Hindu community.[18]

In other words, Innes echoes the dominant view of the colonial establishment that, despite differences of caste and community, the Hindus were a crucial segment of the people constituting the broader population of India.

On the contrary, Nelson's probing account of the Indian people did not allow him to presume a unified religious identity that Innes took for granted. Therefore, the applicability of Anglo-Hindu law, to the extent that it axiomatically applied to any section of the Indian population, could also not be presumed. As Nelson notes, 'there is not, and ... never has been, a Hindu nation or people ... and it would be idle to attempt to discover by research a body of positive laws based in the general consciousness of such a nation or people'.[19]

This radically different account of the Indian people and their customs was a step too far for Innes and others like him in the colonial establishment. Nelson's account of custom could be accepted only to the extent that it comported with and could be absorbed within Anglo-Hindu law. That is, custom could be accepted only as far as it could be conclusively proven and shown to be a stream that emptied into the broader currents of Anglo-Hindu law.[20] Thus, Nelson's challenge ended as a flutter that did little to trouble the Anglo-Hindu tradition of personal law or the conception of the Indian people on which it was established.

Therefore, as the Anglo-Hindu personal law system acquired a measure of stability towards the end of the nineteenth century, it presented itself as axiomatic rules pulling together norms of the people it identified as Hindu. The questions raised by Nelson about the unity of the Hindu people continued to remain. However, having legally collected a significant body of the Indian population under its umbrella, Anglo-Hindu law became a site where emerging national classes could speak on behalf of the Indian people understood as 'Hindus'.

A similar story could be told for what has now become Anglo-Muslim law where communities with disparate customs and usages were pulled together as Muslim.[21] Thus, in the urge to divine the character of the Indian people, classical traditions reflecting on law and ethics were reorganised or mis-recognised as they were mapped onto people that the colonial state called Hindus and Muslims. In turn, as Hindu and Muslim law became well-established pillars of the colonial state, they also presented themselves as axes of social solidarity and Indian political identification. Consequently, as embodiments of the Indian people, personal law become a site where Indians pitched for projects to represent and reform their collective self-interests.

Reform, Personal Law and Indian Self-Expression

As a legal frame that identified Indians as distinct groups of peoples, personal laws offered a unique ground for Indians to speak for, reform and improve their collective lot. The richly layered field of reform studies shows that this effort was informed by and pressed for from various vantage points. These range from the desire to modernise Indian society,[22] assuaging and improving the lot of interest groups to whom personal law applied,[23] as also providing a site from which Indians could take charge of speaking for themselves as national communities.[24]

In the scheme of this book, this mobilisation for reform has been cast as a constituent axis shaping the identity of the Indian people. Thus, drawing on that hypothesis, this section presents personal law as the ground on which Indians came together to demand change for their personal law communities or people. It must of course be mentioned that personal law was not the principal ground on which the project for the reform of Indian society was organised. Reform included a range of concerns, from temple entry, temple dancing, age of consent for consummation of marriages to animal sacrifice, and so on. Personal law reform was only one aspect of this array of concerns, but it certainly was a significant site on which Indians made gradual and piecemeal demands for social reform and change. This manner of reform in fits and starts can be traced to both Hindu and Muslim personal law in the late nineteenth century. Nonetheless, it is Muslim demands for change in their personal law that have been understood as having coherently opened the path for wide-ranging reforms that culminated with Indian independence.[25]

Reform, Legislative Change and the Path to Indian Independence

One of the prominent early efforts to reform Muslim personal law was organised around the recognition of *waqf*s, or Muslim trusts. Through the Waqf Validating Act of 1913, wealthy Muslim families pressed the colonial state to prevent fragmentation of large estates.[26] However, a significant part of the effort to reform Muslim personal law sought to reorganise the widespread recognition of customary practices organising the succession of property in colonial courts. Like Hindu law, Muslim law also recognised a wide patchwork of customs that varied across different provinces and all of which were granted primacy over textual law if they could be proved before a court of law. These customs often fared poorly in defending the rights of women and came in the way of pulling together a unified Muslim nation or people, which became an important concern as the twentieth century wore on. The quest to do away with these customary succession practices for a personal law based on Islamic textual traditions was pursued by Muslim reformers through statutes like the

Mapillah Success Act, 1916, and the Cutchi Memon Act of 1920, culminating with the Shariat Act of 1937.[27]

In the period after the Shariat Act, Muslim reform was overshadowed by efforts to reform Hindu law. This was because the Shariat Act had considerably reorganised and consolidated Muslim law by doing away with various customary succession practices from across the Indian subcontinent in favour of a personal law framework that would apply to all Muslims uniformly.[28] In addition, in the post-independence period (as will be addressed later in this chapter) nationalist consensus believed that it did not have the legitimacy to undertake further reform of Muslim law. That is, it was felt that the impetus for such reform would have to be generated from within the Muslim community, which was difficult to secure from a community viewed to be beleaguered by the partition of British India.

On the other hand, surveying efforts to reform Hindu law, it will be noticed that Hindu reformers did not make any significant impact until the late 1920s. The passage of the Sarda Act in 1929 restrained child marriages, and later the Gains of Learning Act of 1930 made the gains of education the exclusive property of the learner and not of the joint family that might have funded the learning.[29] In addition, inspired by the consolidation of Muslim law by the Shariat Act, a more comprehensive attempt to reorganise Hindu succession laws to improve the rights of women was enacted through the Hindu Women's Right to Property Act, 1937.

Limitations in this latter statute led the government to set up a committee that advised the government to enact a comprehensive Hindu code that would reorganise and reform the fragmented state of Anglo-Hindu law.[30] The recommendations of the committee, as well as broader social pressure for reform, brought about sweeping Hindu law reform in the immediate years after independence. Through a set of four separate statutes, governing Hindu marriage, divorce, inheritance, succession guardianship and adoption, Anglo-Hindu law was reorganised to enlarge the rights of Hindu women, reduce the salience of customary practice and do away with caste-based distinctions that determined the applicability of personal law to different groups of Hindus. As with the Shariat Act, this effort towards the reform of Hindu law consolidated Hindu law such that it would apply to a Hindu people pulled together by these statutes.

As a re-statement of events across the first half of the twentieth century, this summary account of personal law reorganisation and reform foregrounds the consolidation of communities along the religious axes that constituted personal law. Of course, as a legal scheme organised to accommodate religious sentiment, personal law reform could not have been organised in any manner but to foreground religious identity. Even so, it is important to note the widespread adoption of personal laws by India's nationalising elites as a form of identification and Indian self-expression.

At independence, the religious sociology on which personal laws were based passed into the Indian Constitution, presumably through Article 372 which mandated that laws in force in colonial India would continue unless explicitly repealed or altered. However, at the moment of constitutional framing, the case for not altering personal laws and its conception of the Indian people came against other forms of modelling the Indian people – the most powerful of which was the aspiration to establish a liberal secular Constitution founded on the idea that the Indian people were best fashioned as a community of individual citizens. This clash of values had to be mediated at the moment of constitutional founding, and it is to this mediation that this chapter must now turn to as it marks the contours along which the practice of personal law issues in the contemporary Constitution have confronted the identity of the Indian people.

Incorporating Personal Laws into the Indian Constitution: The Assembly Debates

The debate on personal laws in the constitution-making process was largely organised around draft Article 35 in the chapter on directive principles which stated that 'the State shall endeavour to secure for the citizens a uniform civil code throughout the territory of India'. As obvious, this provision embodied a compromise signalling that personal laws would continue into the Constitution of independent India but with the proviso that the state would attempt, when feasible, to do away with them for a uniform civil code.

The Constituent Assembly debates show draft Article 35 weaving a compromise from two different kinds of arguments on the incorporation of personal laws into the constitutional framework of independent India. Those arguing for personal laws, primarily Muslims, made the case that personal law should be understood as part of religious freedom. In addition, having cast religious freedom as the collective right of a people, they argued that any proposal for altering the status quo on personal laws ought not to proceed without the consent of the affected community. On the other hand, those arguing for diminished significance of personal laws in the new Constitution did so by pointing to the inauguration of a new chapter in the history of sovereign secular power. They argued that the new Constitution ought to foreclose older forms of collective identification, like personal laws, which fragmented the unity of the Indian nation to act for the welfare of the Indian people as a whole.

To tease out a flavour of this debate, it is useful to examine and contrast excerpts from this exchange. Thus, arguing for the continuation of personal laws, Mohammad Ismail Khan explicitly linked personal laws to the religious freedoms of Muslims as a people. Accordingly, to him

> the right to follow personal law is part of the way of life of those people who are following such laws; it is part of their religion and part of their culture. If anything is done affecting the personal laws, it will be tantamount to interference with the way of life of those people who have been observing these laws for generations.[31]

Like Khan, all other Muslim members who intervened in the debate on the draft Article understood religious freedom as a collective right that could not be altered without the consent of the community.[32]

The arguments of Muslim members were, however, at odds with the general mood of the house, which was set on granting legislatures the power to replace personal law systems with a uniform civil code. The inspiration for a uniform civil code drew on a general suspicion harboured in the Assembly for all forms of solidarities outside the framework of national unity.[33] This position was well articulated in K. M. Munshi's intervention where he argued for moving towards a uniform civil code stating that

> we must unify and consolidate the nation by every means without interfering with religious practices. If however the religious practices in the past have been so construed as to cover the whole field of life, we have reached a point when we must put our foot down and say that these matters are not religion, they are purely matters for secular legislation.[34]

Defending this assertion of national sovereignty Munshi also pointed to the Shariat Act, which he held up as an analogous example of sovereign power deployed to consolidate Muslim identity, but at the expense of religious practices of communities like the Khojas and Cutchi Memons. Therefore, drawing on the precedent of the Shariat Act and echoing the aspirations of the Assembly, Munshi articulated a vision for the future of personal laws refracted through the prism of secular liberal citizenship and national unity.[35]

Of course, the ambition to shed the religious identities emphasised by personal laws could not hide the fact that the draft Article 35 was only a deferred statement of intent in favour of a uniform civil code. This deferral was especially disappointing to those in the Assembly arguing for significant reform of personal laws to advance a gender-just regulation of family relations that applied uniformly to all citizens.[36] However, Muslim unease over sweeping personal law reform, which also the Assembly took very seriously, pushed the house to adopt draft Article 35 without any changes as Article 44 of the Constitution of India. It is in this manner that Article 44 came to express a scheme for state power that did not fundamentally disturb the organisation of personal law and yet mandated that the state work towards securing a uniform civil code. Consequently, it is the intersection of these different normative visions about personal laws as they have shaped the identity of the Indian people that this chapter must now examine and elaborate.

Interpreting the Constitutional Compromise on Personal Laws

At the cusp of Indian independence the regulation of religious freedom was largely organised along denominational and perhaps even communal lines. Personal laws, whose continuity was tacitly recognised in Article 44, is the best example of this approach to religious regulation. However, this approach also left its mark on a whole range of other religious practices such as temple entry, animal sacrifice and temple dancing, as noted in Chapter 1. In each of these instances state power could have been organised and interpreted to recognise the entitlements of groups in terms consistent with liberal norms. However, state practice has almost without exception fashioned these issues by entrenching denominational or communal rights. Consequently, driven as it was by liberal constitutional desires, would Indian constitutional practice be able to cut through the communal thicket that organised the regulation of personal law?

The *Narasu Appa Mali* Case and Its Legacy

Deferring the ambition to do away with personal laws, India's Constitution makers were resigned to the continued legal recognition of personal laws. However, this did not imply any cessation in efforts to reform personal law.[37] As already noted, the period immediately after independence saw significant reorganisation of Hindu personal law, with the passage of laws bringing about sweeping changes in marriage, divorce, inheritance, succession and guardianship. This was a continuation of a decades-long process of reorganisation of personal law both of Hindus and Muslims understood as separate communities and even as separate peoples. However, in the post-independence period reform was more easily organised for Hindu law as the independent Indian state had the confidence to effect Hindu reform but did not have a similar assurance to speak on behalf of Muslim communities to secure the reform of Muslim law. Similarly, as the debates on the uniform civil code have shown, Muslims who chose to remain in India after partition were clearly on the defensive on matters concerning the reorganisation of personal law which they considered an essential aspect of their religious freedom.

This state of affairs meant that the Indian state was unable to secure the political participation of Muslims in personal law reform after the adoption of the Constitution. In turn, this left the Indian state, broadly committed as it was to the equal application of law, faced with the challenge of justifying what seemed like the asymmetrical application of reform legislation as it applied to different classes of citizens. Relatedly, it was also faced with the broader challenge of tethering personal laws to the guarantees of equal citizenship provided by the Constitution. As political institutions were unable to address these demands, the onus fell on the judiciary. Accordingly, responding to these challenges, the Bombay High Court delivered what continues to be a path-defining decision in *State of Bombay v. Narasu Appa Mali* (*Narasu*).[38]

The *Narasu* case pertained to a constitutional challenge to the Bombay Prevention of Hindu Bigamous Marriages Act, 1946, a statute that penalised Hindu bigamous marriages. This statute was challenged by Hindu parties on grounds that it violated the right to follow religiously enjoined marriage practices, and that it treated communities unequally, especially in singling out Hindus for the reform of their marriage practices. The court's response to these problems can be examined at two levels – first, its response to the constitutionality of the Bombay statute, and second, its account of the constitutionality or the status of personal laws within the new Constitution.

The constitutionality of the Bombay statute was examined through the prism of religious freedom and the charge that the statute violated the constitutional guarantee of equal treatment. Of these, the religious freedom challenge was easily dismissed as the court found that the state clearly had the power to reform religious practices as provided for in Article 25(2). This led to a broader examination of the charge that Hindu marriage practices were asymmetrically singled out for reform in the Bombay statute. This was a stronger charge as the court granted that the Bombay statute was prima facie asymmetrically applied and even discriminatory as a statute designed to apply only to Hindus. However, on closer examination, both judges Chagla and Gajendragadkar, who decided this case, held that this asymmetry was justifiable and did not fall foul of the Constitution. Thus, noting that marriage was understood differently by different communities and that different communities could display different states of preparedness to accept reform legislation, they held there was sufficient ground to justify the Bombay statute's distinction between Hindus and other communities, most notably Muslims.

Related to the constitutionality of the Bombay statute, the court also examined the extent to which aspects of personal law ought to be tied to and subject to the limitations of fundamental rights. This second level at which the *Narasu* court addressed the problem presented to it was a problem that assumed salience against the claims made by the Hindu parties that all personal law practices that derogated from fundamental rights guarantees provided by the Indian Constitution were void to that extent as envisaged by Article 13(1) of the Constitution.

It is possible to argue that the court did not have to answer this question as it had already held that the Bombay statute did not violate the right to religious freedom and the Constitution's equality provisions. However, the court did venture an answer that involved a considerable degree of hair-splitting on whether personal laws could be considered a 'law' subject to the restraint of fundamental rights. This act of legal pedantry is nonetheless extremely significant as it foregrounds the court's understanding of the broader field of personal law and the way it was tied to the writ of law and of the Indian Constitution.

On this score, Justice Gajendragadkar asserted in no uncertain terms that

> [i]t is well-known that the personal laws do not derive their validity on the ground that they have been passed or made by a Legislature or other competent authority in the territory of India. *The foundational sources of both the Hindu and the Mahomedan laws are their respective scriptural texts.*[39] (Emphasis added)

As a self-standing assertion, this position taken by the court is not at all unusual as it merely reiterates the foundational assumptions on which the personal law framework was established in the latter part of the eighteenth century. Nonetheless, as an assertion endorsed by both judges deciding the *Narasu* case, it underscores their peculiar understanding of the place of personal law within the Indian constitutional scheme. That is, they endorse the deeply counter-intuitive idea that the sovereign writ of law embodied in the fundamental rights guarantees stands suspended in the face of religious foundations of personal laws. This opinion becomes more puzzling when placed alongside the court's opinion that legislative authority could reform personal law even though personal laws could not be judicially evaluated against the touchstone of fundamental rights. However, bracketing logical and legal niceties, the court's decision extends the imprimatur of legality to personal laws understood as a unique or *sui generis* species of law. More importantly, in doing so it also recognises and foregrounds the communal conceptualisation of the Indian people on which the colonial state originally founded personal laws – that is, as a people founded on and divided by religious doctrine. Paradoxically, *Narasu* permits this communally organised conceptualisation of the Indian people to coexist, albeit uneasily, with the idea of the Indian people understood as a community of equal citizens.

In a constitutional scheme founded on equal citizenship the *Narasu* decision is doubly puzzling as it has not yet been reversed. In fact, subsequent decisions have only echoed *Narasu's* holding and the fault lines on which it is organised.[40] However, in a recent five-judge constitution bench decision in *Shayara Bano v. Union of India*,[41] one among a plurality of decisions delivered by the Supreme Court displayed willingness to exert a measure of critical constitutional scrutiny over matters pertaining to and arising out of personal law.

In *Shayara Bano* the Supreme Court was petitioned to consider the constitutionality of triple *talaq*, a form of divorce in Muslim personal law that permitted Muslim men to summarily divorce their wives after uttering the word *talaq* three times. The Supreme Court declared the practice to be unconstitutional. However, their decision is significant to this discussion not for the outcome they fashioned but for the reasoning of two judges who held that personal law practices like triple *talaq* ought to be subject to the court's fundamental rights review. Though their reasoning was a movement away from the position carved out in *Narasu*, it did not have the backing of the full court. Nonetheless, it is useful to consider this minority decision as it helps evaluate the extent to which this minority decision could play a role in displacing the colonially and communally inspired conceptualisation of personal law that made *Narasu* possible.

To locate this minority decision against the broader holding of the court in this case, it is helpful to start with the other decisions as they held on the applicability of fundamental rights to matters of personal law. Judges Nazeer and Keher held that personal laws embody the essential and constitutionally protected religious doctrines of religious communities. Unlike the *Narasu* ruling on this question, which attempted to technically insulate personal laws from the scrutiny of fundamental rights on grounds that it was not law under Article 13, Judges Nazeer and Keher attempted to explicitly link the immunity of personal laws with the constitutional right to religious freedom. That is, they argued that the '"personal law" of every religious denomination, is protected from invasion and breach, except as provided by and under Article 25'.[42]

From a strictly doctrinal point of view it could be argued that this is an instance of incorrect legal reasoning as it is unclear if individual right to practise religion under Article 25 includes the right of a religious community to their personal law.[43] However, assuming personal laws to be protected by Article 25, it would follow that personal laws could be reviewed on grounds of public order health and morality, none of which they argued applied in this case. Further, they argued that the Shariat Act, which made Muslim personal law and practices like *talaq* the applicable law to Indian Muslims, ought to be understood as a legislative measure that removed the applicability of customs on Muslim Law and not as a sovereign Act that proactively made the Shariat the applicable law. Collectively, these were the grounds on which they argued that the practice of *talaq* was constitutionally protected. However, their decision did not address *Narasu* and its account of personal law.

Judge Joseph, the third judge who made up the majority position on the constitutionality of triple *talaq*, agreed with Judges Keher and Nazeer on the legal status of triple *talaq* but disagreed that *talaq* was protected by the applicable rules of the Shariat on the question of *talaq*. That is, on the strength of earlier personal law rulings on the status of triple *talaq* in Islamic law, he decided that the practice was not legally permissible. Consequently, identifying *talaq* as flowing from scriptural law, he held along the lines of the *Narasu* decision that the practice was not amenable to the evaluation of fundamental rights. However, neither Judges Kehar and Nazeer nor Judge Joseph pointedly examined the manner in which personal laws ought or ought not to be subject to fundamental rights review.

On the other hand, the decision of Judges Nariman and Lalit brought the practice of triple *talaq* under the evaluative scrutiny of fundamental rights though without directly confronting the legacy of *Narasu*. They did so by including triple *talaq* as a legal artefact governed by the exercise of sovereign power under the Shariat Act of 1937. The Shariat Act stated: 'Notwithstanding any custom or usage to the contrary ... regarding ... marriage, dissolution of marriage, including talaq, ila, zihar, lian, khula, and mubaraat ... the rule of decision in cases where parties are Muslims shall be the Muslim Personal Law (Shariat).'[44] Having thereby classified *talaq* as a practice recognised by statute, it followed that the practice could be scrutinised and rendered consistent with the Constitution and fundamental rights. This task was undertaken by drawing on the Supreme Court's equality jurisprudence and by holding triple *talaq* as a constitutionally impermissible arbitrary practice as it permitted husbands to wield whimsical and capricious power over wives without giving marriages a chance of reconciliation and repair.[45]

As this was a line of reasoning that could have also been adopted in the *Narasu* case, it is important to note the significant normative shift made by Nariman's and Lalit's decision to hold personal law subject to fundamental rights. In *Narasu* the judges made an important distinction between personal law and custom and interpreted the Shariat Act as a statute whose purpose was to remove the salience of custom in Muslim personal law. Even though this is a specious distinction, it permitted the judges in *Narasu* to hold that customs could be subject to constitutional scrutiny but not personal law, which they argued was founded on scriptural authority. Significantly, a version of this argument has travelled all the way from *Narasu* right up to *Shayara Bano* in the decisions of Judges Nazeer, Keher and Joseph. Nariman and Lalit deny the Shariat Act this otherworldly scriptural authority, and it is this move that permitted them to unequivocally bring the statute under the sway of the Constitution and its fundamental rights.

Even as the decision of Nariman and Lalit was an advance on *Narasu*, there are notable instances to which their decision does not apply. For instance, both Judges Nariman and Lalit do not indicate how their decision would apply to personal law practices categorically excluded by the Shariat Act (for example, succession practices related to agricultural land) as it was originally enacted.[46] Similarly, the very applicability of the Shariat Act was tied to a declaration on the part of the concerned parties that they consented to the application of provisions of the Act. Subjecting these excluded situations to the scrutiny of fundamental rights would require a thorough re-examination and reversal of the position in the *Narasu* case that immunised all instances of personal law not otherwise specified by statute from the scrutiny of fundamental rights. Though Judges Nariman and Lalit cast doubt on the correctness of *Narasu*, they did not pronounce on the matter as they arrived at their decision independent of the holding in *Narasu*.

Thus, to summarise this discussion, judicial doctrine on the constitutionality of personal law continues to echo *Narasu*, and through *Narasu* the view that personal law embodies the axiomatic scriptural truth of a religious community or people that is beyond constitutional control. It is of course possible that a future court could draw on the advance made by Nariman and Lalit to treat personal law as a legal artefact that ensues from state authority to make it subject to the fundamental rights guaranteed by the Constitution. This would also displace the sociology of India and Indians as a community or people pulled together by axiomatic scriptural truths that *Narasu* presumes.

Of course, the displacement of the position in *Narasu* does not necessarily imply the supplanting of personal laws, as the privileges permitted by personal law for various religious groups could be rendered consistent with the fundamental rights of all citizens. That is, personal law could continue as a form of multicultural group rights.[47] On the other hand, if there is a concerted movement towards a uniform civil code, this would imply that constitutional law and its parctice would have pushed aside the role that personal laws have played in organising personal relations between Indians. Movement towards either of these outcomes is by no means certain but is constrained by the Communal Constitution and its conception of the Indian people.

As Chapter 1 has shown and as this book will show across its chapters, the Communal Constitution frames the Indian people in axiomatically organised scriptural or doctrinal terms across different aspects or domains of the Constitution. In addition, the Communal Constitution also interlocks different parts of the Constitution to collectively reiterate the Communal Constitution. Thus, even as it is possible to see a glimmer of a liberal constitutional vision in decisions of judges like Nariman and Lalit, this liberal conception of the people is also confronted by the collective clasp of other facets of the Communal Constitution. In this regard it is perhaps also useful to point to a communally pointed exasperation through which the Indian higher judiciary has vented its frustration and even fury against Muslims for standing the way of a uniform civil code as directed by Article 44 of the Constitution.

Uniform Civil Code as a Jurisprudence of Exasperation

Across this chapter, personal laws have been roughly framed around two poles. One pole collected personal laws as colonially organised and scripturally inspired axioms or doctrines that were pulled together as the laws of a people. The other cast personal laws as legal artefacts that draw on religious resources but whose authority is determined and limited as recognised by sovereign state power. These poles and the points of view attached to them have presented themselves in various discussions that have been highlighted in this and previous chapters.

Thus, as the colonial state treated personal laws as the foundational religious norms of its Hindu and Muslim subjects, the challenge posed by James Nelson viewed personal laws as a system of laws misapplied by colonial state power. Similarly, as reform deepened the attachment of Indians to an axiomatically and scripturally grounded conception of personal law, the aspirations of an independent India viewed personal laws as a legal form that the new state ought to be able to reorder and change in the exercise of its sovereign will. The Indian Constitution sought to strike a compromise between these positions in Article 44 by recognising and even directing the use of state power to displace personal law, but leaving the appropriate moment for such change to the judgement of a future government.

However, there have been few credible initiatives, either political or institutional, to reorder personal laws to secure a uniform civil code. Against this background, a set of widely known Supreme Court decisions have intervened in the discussion on personal laws with acerbic observations on the failure to move towards a uniform civil code. This section highlights the effects of these Supreme Court decisions and the way they reinforce the communal foundations of personal laws even while seeming to push against them.

Thus, in *Mohd. Ahmed Khan v. Shah Bano Begam*[48] the Supreme Court had to decide the extent to which the jurisdiction of personal laws was tied to the general writ of criminal law in cases where they came into direct conflict. The technical detail of the case concerned the application of Section 125 of the Code of Criminal Procedure, which cast an obligation on all husbands with sufficient means to maintain estranged wives who were unable to maintain themselves. The appellant in this case challenged a demand made by his divorced wife under this section on grounds that he had made all required payments on divorce as obliged by Muslim personal and was required to make no further payment. Drawing on the Code of Criminal Procedure, the court held that Muslim personal law could not supersede the statute and that the husband was obliged to pay maintenance to his wife as mandated by Section 125.

If the Supreme Court had stuck to narrowly resolving this question, this case would have disappeared into the ocean of litigation that patched many such aspects of family conflict. However, this was not to be as the court made two important moves to address the reluctance of Muslim litigants in the case to accede to the authority of Section 125 of the Code of Criminal Procedure. First, it framed and explained the problem of maintenance of wives unable to maintain themselves as consistent with Islamic religious doctrine. Second, and more importantly for the present discussion, the court pushed the state to address the 'disparate loyalties' of Muslims attached to their personal laws by working towards a uniform civil code.[49]

These observations by the court formed part of a chain of events that culminated in the demolition of the Babri Majid that deeply polarised Indian polity and which has been discussed at length in Chapter 1. To reconstruct this turn of events briefly, the decision in *Shah Bano* ruffled the sensibilities of influential sections within the Muslim community which were in turn assuaged by the then government with the passage of the Muslim Women (Protection on Divorce Act) in 1986. This statute reversed the holding of the *Shah Bano* case and held that customary payments in Muslim personal law would supersede the obligation of husbands to maintain wives as provided in Section 125 of the criminal code. The statute was met with protest by Hindu groups alleging preferential treatment for Muslims, prompting the government's decision to open the locks of the Ram Janmabhoomi–Babri Masjid complex. Eventually this rush to balance wounded sentiments of different communities failed and perhaps even fuelled the chain of events leading to the demolition of the Babri Masjid.

Against this background it is difficult not to notice that the court's observations on Islamic doctrine and the uniform civil code were entirely gratuitous and superfluous to the legal question brought for resolution before the court. That is, questions about the uniform civil code were entirely superfluous to decisions about the extent and manner in which personal law was to accede to the criminal code where they were in conflict. On the other hand, the court's gratuitous remarks on the loyalty of Muslims as citizens of the Indian republic only deepened fissures as they cascaded into epoch-making conflicts as in the clash over the Ram Janmabhoomi–Babri Masjid complex. *Shah Bano* was, however, not an aberration – other cases attacked personal law and Muslim loyalties with greater vehemence.

In *Sarla Mudgal v. Union of India*,[50] the Supreme Court was presented with a set of petitions challenging the conversion of Hindu men to the Islamic faith to enter a second marriage when their first marriage remained undissolved. Legally the problem required the court to examine whether a Hindu man married under Hindu law could embrace Islam to solemnise a valid second marriage. Relatedly, the court also examined whether a husband who contracted a second marriage in this fashion would be guilty of the offence of bigamy as detailed in Section 494 of the Indian Penal Code.

The court answered these doctrinal questions holding that the second marriage claiming privileges of Islamic law would have no impact on the first marriage contracted under Hindu law. Consequently, the second marriage contracted without dissolution of the first would be void and illegal according to the provisions of the Hindu Marriage Act. In turn, the attempt to contract the second marriage was held a bigamous marriage prohibited by Section 494 of the Indian Penal Code. The court needed to have said no more to resolve the problems raised by this case. However, as in *Shah Bano*, this case also became a channel to voice the court's misgivings about Muslims, Muslim personal law and the urgency to work towards a uniform civil code.

To Judge Kuldeep Singh, the problem this case showed up was the inadequate progress made towards the reform of Muslim personal law. However, even as it is true that independent India has not made any significant effort towards the reform of Muslim law, the judge makes an entirely unexplained jump from the reform of Muslim law to the need for a uniform civil code. Intriguingly, he does so by comparing the lack of reform in Muslim law with the reform and codification of Hindu law in the 1950s. Most significantly, the codification of Hindu law is also described as a step towards securing a uniform civil code. As he narrated the problem,

> when more than 80% of the citizens have already been brought under the codified personal law there is no justification whatsoever to keep in abeyance, any more, the introduction of 'uniform civil code' for all citizens in the territory of India.[51]

The 80 per cent of the citizenry praiseworthily identified are the Hindus, Sikhs, Buddhists and Jains to whom the Hindu Code applied. This account of a communally organised (Hindu) reform effort is explained as an advance towards a uniform civil code. In turn, he also pronounces the end that he seeks, the uniform civil code, as being frustrated by Muslims who refuse to give up their personal law even against the Constitution's demand to do so in Article 44.

Kuldeep Singh's diatribe is unrelenting, questioning the loyalties of Muslims by reminding the community that

> [t]hose who preferred to remain in India after the partition, fully knew that the Indian leaders did not believe in two-nation or three-nation theory and that in the Indian Republic there was to be only one Nation – the Indian nation – and no community could claim to remain a separate entity on the basis of religion.[52]

Finally, having got his homily out of the way, all that remained for Kuldeep Singh was to remind the government that they also had a constitutional duty to make every effort to secure this code as soon as possible. Like in *Shah Bano*, it is remarkable that these observations in *Sarla Mudgal* had no conceivable bearing on the cases that were brought to the court for resolution. Further, it is important to note that both these cases form part of a line of decisions where the courts digressed from the doctrinal legal problems that had to be resolved to exhort governments to take action to secure a uniform civil code.[53] Some cases were less strident towards minorities when compared to *Shah Bano* and *Sarla Mudgal*; even so, all cases share in a common judicial exasperation at the inability to secure a uniform civil code.

The exasperation that courts have repeatedly shown on the lack of progress towards a uniform code has, however, not been accompanied by a concrete sense of what a uniform civil code would entail. Thus, from the constitutional recognition granted to the customary practices of north-eastern tribal communities, the customary practices recognised within the codified Hindu law, the normative shortcomings within the existing personal law schemes, to fears that a uniform civil code could result in a largely Hindu code, there are a range of concerns that a uniform civil code would have to address and resolve.[54] Further, as Judge Sahai pointed out in a separate decision alongside Kuldeep Singh in *Sarla Mudgal*, a uniform civil code could not be secured without also attempting to secure a degree of consensus in all communities on the need to move towards a mutually agreeable code.[55] However, few of these concerns are considered in the judicial exasperation on the inability of the Indian state to achieve a uniform civil code.

Thus, even as the judicial push for a uniform civil code is driven by the goal of equal citizenship, the confrontational form in which it has been articulated has only amplified the representation of the Indian people as constituted and divided by religious identity. Courts have of course also mirrored Hindu nationalist politics in singling out Muslims, whose personal law practices have been characterised as incompatible with equal citizenship. In fact, as scholars have pointed out, the lack of reform among Muslims for problems such as polygamy or destitution of wives, the issues at stake in *Shah Bano* and *Sarla Mudgal*, is as much a problem in many other communities.[56] However, it is not so much the animus against Muslims that this chapter has sought to highlight as the deeply set conceptualisation of the Indian people on which it draws. That is, even when the court seeks to act to further seemingly secular values, it is driven by a political sociology that casts India and Indians as boxed into and divided by communal identities.

Therefore, by reiterating this communalising strand of constitutional imagination as it has taken hold of the organisation and practice of personal law, this chapter pulls together its conclusion.

Conclusion

Thus, in conclusion, this chapter has sought to elaborate and echo the argument of Chapter 1 that a doctrinally and axiomatically organised conceptualisation of religion forms an integral part of the manner in which the Indian Constitution models its people. Across colonial and postcolonial India, this chapter shows that this communal characterisation and division of the Indian people continue to be a powerful way of approaching the place of personal law in contemporary Indian law.

Constitutional design in independent India has tried to trace an alternative path for personal laws that could potentially cast this legal domain through the prism of group rights or even dispense with personal laws in favour of a uniform civil code. However, a colonial and communal form of understanding personal laws continues to shape constitutional practice, echoing the communal constitutional image of the Indian people that was identified in Chapter 1. As mentioned previously, the power of the communal conceptualisation of the Indian people is not just its presence in discrete parts of the Constitution or in unconnected constitutional debates. On the contrary, the book seeks to argue that the Communal Constitution is reiterated and echoed across many aspects of constitutional organisation. More importantly, each reiteration of this communal conceptualisation of the Indian people is interlocked with other instances to produce India's Communal Constitution. Accordingly, other instances of the Communal Constitution as it is present and woven into debates on minority rights and caste identity are elaborated in subsequent chapters.

Notes

1. For example, see Judge Chandrachud in *Mohd. Ahmed Khan v. Shah Bano Begam* MANU/SC/0194/1985.
2. For example, see Tahir Mahmood, *Uniform Civil Code: Fictions and Facts* (New Delh: India and Islam Research Council, 1995).
3. For example, see Cohn, 'Law and the Colonial State in India'; Anderson, 'Islamic Law and the Colonial Encounter'; Lariviere, 'Justices and Panditas'; Asif, *The Loss of Hindustan*.

4.   J. Duncan M. Derrett, 'The British as Patrons of the Sastra', *Religion, Law and the State in India*, ed. J. D. M. Derrett, 225–74 (New Delhi: Oxford University Press, 1999).

5.   Robert Lingat, *The Classical Law of India* (New edn, New Delhi: Oxford University Press, 1998), x–xiii, 3.

6.   See Lingat, *The Classical Law of India*; Donald R. Davis, *The Spirit of Hindu Law* (Reprint edn, Cambridge, UK: Cambridge University Press, 2013), 1–25.

7.   Davis, *The Spirit of Hindu Law*, 13.

8.   Derrett, 'The British as Patrons of the Sastra'.

9.   Derrett, 'The British as Patrons of the Sastra'; Davis, *The Spirit of Hindu Law*.

10. See Purohit, *The Aga Khan Case*.

11. See Mallampalli, *Race, Religion and Law in Colonial India*.

12. For the most important of Nelson's work, see J. H. Nelson, *A View of the Hindu Law as Administered by the High Court of Judicature at Madras* (Madras: Higginbotham & Co., 1877); J. H. Nelson, *Indian Usage and Judge Made Law in Madras* (London: Kegan Paul & Co., 1887); J. H. Nelson, *A Prospectus of the Scientific Study of the Hindû Law* (London: Kegan Paul & Co., 1881). See also J. Duncan M. Derrett, 'J. H. Nelson: A Forgotten Administrator-Historian of India', inHistorians of India, Pakistan and Ceylon, ed. Cyril Henry Philips, 354–72 (London: Oxford University Press 1961).

13. Nelson, *A View of the Hindu Law as Administered by the High Court of Judicature at Madras*, iii.

14. Nelson, *A View of the Hindu Law as Administered by the High Court of Judicature at Madras*, iii, 1.

15. Nelson traces this commitment to toleration to authorities ranging from charter of the Supreme Court, the Madras Regulation of 1802, the Madras Civil Courts Act, 1873 as well as the Queen's proclamation of 1858 after the Indian revolt. Nelson, *Indian Usage and Judge Made Law in Madras*, 7–8.

16. Refuting his critique Justice Innes of the Madras implored the government to reject his suggestions. Innes, *Examination of Mr. Nelson's Views of Hindu Law*.

17. Innes, *Examination of Mr. Nelson's Views of Hindu Law*, 96, 98–103.

18. Innes, *Examination of Mr. Nelson's Views of Hindu Law*, 11.

19. Nelson, *A View of the Hindu Law as Administered by the High Court of Judicature at Madras*, 11.

20. For example, see Dwarka Nath Mitter, *Position of Women in Hindu Law*, vol. 1 (New Delhi: Cosmo Publications, 2006) 40; John Dawson Mayne, *A Treatise on Hindu Law and Usage* (7th edn, Madras: Higginbotham & Co., 1906), 46. See also Srikantan, *Identifying and Regulating Religion in India*, 18–62.

21. Srikantan, *Identifying and Regulating Religion in India*, 62–93.

22. For example, see Lucy Carroll, 'Law, Custom, and Statutory Social Reform: The Hindu Widows' Remarriage Act of 1856', *Indian Economic and Social History Review* 20, no. 4 (1983): 363.

23. For example, see Eleanor Newbigin, 'The Codification of Personal Law and Secular Citizenship', *Indian Economic and Social History Review* 46, no. 1 (2009): 83.

24. Chatterjee, *The Nation and Its Fragments*.

25. Newbigin, 'The Codification of Personal Law and Secular Citizenship'.

26. Newbigin, 'The Codification of Personal Law and Secular Citizenship'. See also Gregory C. Kozlowski, *Muslim Endowments and Society in British India* (Cambridge, UK: Cambridge University Press, 2008).

27. See George Rankin, 'Custom and the Muslim Law in British India', *Transactions of the Grotius Society* 25 (1939): 89.

28. See Rina Verma Williams, *Postcolonial Politics and Personal Laws: Colonial Legal Legacies and the Indian State* (New Delhi: Oxford University Press, 2006); Sen, *Articles of Faith*.

29. Williams, *Postcolonial Politics and Personal Laws*; Newbigin, 'The Codification of Personal Law and Secular Citizenship'.

30. Chitra Sinha, *Debating Patriarchy: The Hindu Code Bill Controversy in India* (New Delhi: Oxford University Press, 2012).

31. 'Constituent Assembly Debates', 23rd November 1948, Vol. 7, Doc. 58, Para 108, https://www.constitutionofindia.net/constitution_assembly_debates/volume/7/1948-11-23, accessed 9 December 2021.

32. See speeches by Naziruddin Ahmad, B. Pocker Sahib Bahadur and Hussain Imam, 'Constituent Assembly Debates', 23rd November 1948, Vol. 7, Doc. 58, Para 108.

33. See Ambedkar and Munshi's draft fundamental rights articles which attempted to marginalise the salience of personal laws. Partha S. Ghosh, *The Politics of Personal Law in South Asia: Identity, Nationalism and the Uniform Civil Code* (New Delhi: Routledge India, 2007), 65.

34. 'Constituent Assembly Debates', 23rd November 1948, Vol. 7, Doc. 58, Para. 147.

35. 'Constituent Assembly Debates', 23rd November 1948, Vol. 7, Doc. 58, Para. 147.

36. Ghosh, *The Politics of Personal Law in South Asia*, 65–66.

37. For an account of such reform efforts in judicial interpretation, see Werner Menski, 'The Uniform Civil Code Debate in Indian Law: New Developments and Changing Agenda', *German Law Journal* 9 (2008): 211.

38. *State of Bombay v. Narasu Appa Mali* MANU/MH/0040/1952 (hereafter *Narasu*).

39. *Narasu*, para 20.

40. See decisions in *Harvinder Kaur v Harminder Singh* AIR 1984 Del 66; *Saroj Rani v Sudarshan* AIR 1984 SC 1562l.

41. *Shayara Bano v. Union of India and Ors.* MANU/SC/1031/2017.

42. *Shayara Bano v. Union of India and Ors.*, para 146.

43. Gautam Bhatia, 'The Supreme Court's Triple Talaq Judgment', *Indian Constitutional Law and Philosophy*, 22 August 2017, https://indconlawphil. wordpress.com/2017/08/22/the-supreme-courts-triple-talaq-judgment/, accessed 10 December 2021.

44. Section 2.

45. *Shayara Bano v. Union of India and Ors.*, para 45.

46. See Williams, *Postcolonial Politics and Personal Laws*.

47. Menski, 'The Uniform Civil Code Debate in Indian Law'.

48. MANU/SC/0194/1985.

49. In particular, see *Mohd. Ahmed Khan v. Shah Bano*, para 32.

50. *Sarla Mudgal v. Union of India* MANU/SC/0290/1995.

51. *Sarla Mudgal v. Union of India*, para 1.

52. *Sarla Mudgal v. Union of India*, para 33.

53. *John Vallamattom v. Union of India*, 6 SCC 611 (2003); *Jose Paulo Coutinho v. Maria Luiza Valentina Pereira* (2019) SCC ONLINE SC 1190; *Jordan Diengdeh v. S.S. Chopra* AIR 1985 SC 935.

54. Alok Prasanna Kumar, 'Uniform Civil Code: A Heedless Quest?' *Economic and Political Weekly* 51, no. 25 (2015): 7.

55. *Sarla Mudgal v. Union of India*, paras 41–42.

56. Flavia Agnes, 'Hindu Men, Monogamy and Uniform Civil Code' *Economic and Political Weekly* 30, no. 52 (1995): 3238. See also Flavia Agnes, 'Has the Codified Hindu Law Changed Gender Relationships?' *Social Change* 46, no. 4 (2016): 611.

3

A Lurking Majoritarianism

A Communal Account of Minority Rights

This chapter extends the axiomatically and scripturally organised depiction of the Indian people developed in earlier chapters to the problem of representation and self-government. Doing so, the emphasis of enquiry shifts from religion and religious identity as objects of government to religious identity as it has organised and structured the contours of the Indian state. This shift in emphasis is framed by the third of the three constituent axes that structure this book – namely forms of political representation that originated in colonial India that continue to inflect contemporary constitutional government. Accordingly, this chapter on minority rights and the following chapter on caste identity detail the communal representation of the Indian people across colonial and contemporary constitutional practice.

To ascertain the continuing imprint of a communally imagined people on the organisation of minority rights, this chapter is divided into three sections. First, an outline of minority rights in the colonial state. Second, an examination of the recessed communal form through which minority rights were reworked and inserted into the Constitution of independent India. Third, the continuing imprint of this communal conceptualisation of the Indian people in contemporary constitutional practice.

The Pedagogical Foundations of Indian Constitutionalism

Minority rights were the very ground on which the British colonial state shaped representative politics for India in the late nineteenth and early twentieth centuries. The constitutional contours of minority rights unfolded over this period through a series of constitutional statutes, most notably the Indian Councils Act ,1909, the Government of India Act, 1919, and the Government of India Act, 1935. Each of these statutes drew large numbers of Indians into the British government and also set the path for the subsequent organisation of the Indian government. Further, when the Constitution of independent India was adopted, a significant part of the new institutional arrangement drew on the earlier Government of India Act of 1935. However, continuities in constituent imagination do not just narrate the endurance of institutional frames and practices, but the survival of forms through which a polity carves out and makes salient its people. It is this dimension of minority rights that must now be outlined.

To cut through much historical detail, the colonial template framing a constituent horizon for modern India was first organised as a project of 'trust' whose goal was the transfer of power to the Indian people.[1] The colonial administrator and historian Reginald Coupland traces the influence of trust as an animating idea in Indian government all the way back to the thought of Edmund Burke. Burke noted that Englishmen have never supposed that India's

> subjection to British rule, however long it might last, was a permanent dispensation. The ultimate enfranchisement of India was implicit in Burke's doctrine of trusteeship, since the guardian's duty ends once his ward comes of age.[2]

The legacy of Burke, as Coupland homes in on it, was a recurring theme in colonial justifications of rule in India. It could be maintained that this imprint has already been highlighted in previous chapters in the disposition of the colonial state to tolerate and to govern Indians by guaranteeing their religious laws, truths and freedoms. However, in organising colonial institutions, the idea of trust was tied to the perception that India's socio-political backwardness demanded a colonially led project of political education to enable Indian subjects to take charge of their own government. Thus, for instance, in discussions on the charter of 1833, T.B. Macaulay would argue that

by good government we may educate our subjects into a capacity for better government;
that, having become instructed in European knowledge, they may, in some future age,
demand European institutions. Whether such a day will ever come I know not.
But never will I attempt to avert or to retard it. Whenever it comes, it will be the
proudest day in English history. To have found a great people sunk in the lowest
depths of slavery and superstition, to have so ruled them as to have made them
desirous and capable of all the privileges of citizens, would indeed be a title to
glory all our own.[3] (Emphasis added)

The ultimate object and even legitimacy of the political education of India's
'sunken' people was therefore presented as self-rule via universal citizenship
organised in the image of European politics. As these ideas legitimating
colonial rule found expression in constitutional statutes across the latter part
of the nineteenth and the early twentieth centuries, Indian backwardness
was concretely identified as the problem of irreconcilable social division and
the consequent inability to express a unified political will. In turn, the lack
of a political will was to be an important driver of the British constituent
imagination for India.

To illustrate the presumption of social division in an early constitutional
statute, Lord Landsdowne introduced the Indian Councils Act of 1892 as set
against the background of a society that he described as 'congeries of widely
separated classes races and communities, with divergences of interests and
hereditary sentiments which for ages have precluded common sentiment or
local unanimity'.[4] This assumption has been of great significance to the colonial
state in India in the first half of the twentieth century as the conceptualisation
of an irreconcilably divided society was grafted onto the making of government.
That is, communal or sectarian difference, and especially religious difference,
became an important criterion for incorporating Indian participation in
colonial government.

By extension, it was through government organised in these communal
terms that the obligation of political education or trust was discharged. Set
against such inhospitable conditions it was difficult to conceive of Indian
political unity, which was the purported end of colonial pedagogy. Nonetheless,
it was against the shadow of this judgement about India and its people that
constitutional institutions took shape in colonial India.

The institutionalisation of communal difference was made principally
possible through a variety of separate and divided electorates that organised
a limited but gradually expanding franchise for Indians in the British
government. This scheme for enfranchising Indians was instituted on a

pan-Indian level through the Indian Councils Act of 1909.[5] As a milestone in British constitutional government in India, this statute was premised on the belief that Indians were at this point largely unprepared for self-rule and that it was only possible to permit a minimal representation of various community interests that were otherwise different in 'life, in tradition, in history, in all the social things as well as articles of belief that constitute a community'.[6] As part of this accommodation of Indian interests, the Muslim community was perhaps the most prominent of the social groups whose interests were identified for representation through the form of a separate electorate.

Preparing ground for the next major constitutional re-organisation, the Government of India Act of 1919, the Montagu–Chelmsford report proposed considerable constitutional reform and the greater inclusion of Indians in the government of British India. The report also made a strong case for moving towards unified national citizenship and thereby to pull back from the sectarian conception of representation instituted in 1909. However, despite these intentions, the report expressed helplessness at reworking the framework of separate electorates as it felt that it could not resile from earlier privileges granted to groups such as the Muslims.[7] In fact, the 1919 Act actually went on to extend separate electorates to more groups such as the Sikhs, Marathas, non-Brahmins, Indian Christians, Anglo-Indians, Depressed Classes, large landholders and commercial interests.[8] Thus, even though unified citizenship for all Indians was established as a normative goal by the report, there was no significant change in the assumptions it made about the divided character of Indian society.

To illustrate from the Montagu–Chelmsford report's characterisation of Indian society, it was believed that 'there runs through Indian society a series of cleavages – of religion, race, and caste which constantly threaten its solidarity, and of which any wise political scheme must take serious heed'.[9] Thus, even though the 1919 Act took the view that communal differences threatened 'social solidarity' and the emergence of a unified political will, the conceptualisation of Indian society as irreconcilably divided remained unchanged. Consequently, the framework of separate and divided electorates also remained undisturbed. A principal difference brought in by this constitutional statute, however, was a change in terminology where the communities granted separate electorates or nominated by the government to be represented in colonial legislatures were now termed 'minorities'.[10]

It is important to note that this communal view of minorities was not restricted to religious groups alone and included a range of other identities also understood by the colonial state as constituting the Indian body politic.

However, religion was arguably the oldest of these identities through which the colonial state constituted their view of India. In turn, this was perhaps reflected in the very early recognition of Muslims as one of the most significant of the minorities in the Indian body politic. Therefore, despite asserting political unity and universal citizenship as a normative goal, the recognition and representation of all factional or minority interests became an established feature of Indian constitutional politics.

The problem of representing minorities only multiplied by the time of the next round of political changes leading up to the Government of India Act, 1935, with an increasing number of groups vying to be recognised as such. No discussion of the problem of accommodating minorities is complete without a mention of the momentous confrontation resolved by the Poona Pact in 1932 where Depressed Classes (as lower-caste groups were then called) demanded to be recognised as a distinct minority[11] and be granted a separate electorate. The Poona Pact will be discussed in greater detail in the next chapter when addressing caste and its imprint on Indian constitutional identity. However, for the present discussion it is sufficient to note that the proposal to grant separate electorates to Depressed Classes, led by B. R. Ambedkar, under the Government of India Act ,1935, was staunchly opposed by M. K. Gandhi and the Congress party, leading eventually to the pact between the contending parties.

Under the terms of the Poona Pact, the Depressed Classes were incorporated into Indian constitutional politics, via the Government of India Act of 1935, through special quotas in a joint electorate and not through separate electorates as they then demanded.[12] Even so, they continued to be termed and understood as minorities within the framework of the colonial state and eligible for privileges due to minorities.

Holding off detailed comment on this very important constitutional development for Chapter 4, it is useful to mention that the confrontation resolved by the Poona Pact foregrounds an instance of nationalist striving that attempted to set aside accounts Indian society founded on irreconcilable social division. Nationalists bristled at the pedagogical backdrop against which the colonial state bemoaned Indian disunity or even goaded Indians towards unity. Even so, there was significant consensus within organisations like the Congress on the pedagogical goal of national unity. Consequently, it is possible to view the contentious resolution of the Poona Pact as an illustration of the nationalist approach towards reorganising minority rights guided by the goal of national unity.

The resolution expressed in the Poona Pact pushed the caste question to the background of the other major minority demand – the growing demand for Pakistan that eventually resulted in the partition of British India on religious lines. Partition was clearly a failure of the nationalist imagination that sought to forge a united political identity which could subsume Indian social differences. Equally, it was also a failure of the colonial pedagogical model that projected political unity as the future of constitutional politics in India. Nonetheless, partition was perhaps an inevitable consequence of the communal organisation of the Indian government. Even so, partition pole-vaulted the Indian National Congress to the forefront of constitution making for what was soon to be the independent Indian republic. The Congress expectedly pushed to rework the framework of minority rights in the Constitution that they had inherited from the colonial state towards a political community founded on national unity and equal citizenship. However, as the next sections will argue, despite their best efforts, aspects of the colonial scheme of minority rights were carried into the Constitution of independent India.

A New Conception of Minority Rights: National Unity and the Transformation of the Colonial Constitution

The Congress-led nationalists who came to steer the Indian Constituent Assembly viewed the communal representation of India and her people as a colonial contrivance aimed at preventing the realisation of what they felt was a nation ready to take charge of its destiny. They argued that the communal division upon which the colonial state founded its ideas of India only deepened what were otherwise benign social differences making up a plural but united people. For instance, Govind Ballabh Pant outlined the minority question before the Constituent Assembly in the following manner:

> [T]he question of minorities everywhere looms large in constitutional discussions. Many a constitution has foundered on this rock ... *It has been used so far for creating strife, distrust and cleavage between the different sections of the Indian nation. Imperialism thrives on such strife.* It is interested in fomenting such tendencies. So far, the minorities have been incited and have been influenced in a manner which has hampered the growth of cohesion and unity.[13] (Emphasis added)

In Pant's account, ordinary social divisions between 'sections of the Indian nation' were accentuated by the mischievous designs of imperial government. Consequently, as the constitutional goal of national unity was now within reach, nationalists like Pant set themselves the task of pushing aside the colonial depiction of India as a nation of irreconcilable minorities.

It is important to note, however, that as much as colonial *realpolitik* accentuated schisms between different classes and sections of Indians, Indian social division was also a deeply ingrained intellectual orientation in the colonial government.[14] Further, while attacking the malign designs of the colonial government, those like Pant also shared the pedagogical goals that the colonial state set for India. In other words, it could be said that Pant's attack on the colonial state was targeted not at its stated goal that the plurality in Indian society ought to become 'a people' but at its judgement that Indians could not overcome their differences towards that end. Therefore, it is significant to note that despite their different judgements about the character of Indian social divisions, both the nationalists and the colonial government were united by a common constituent horizon that viewed self-rule as the goal that ought to direct the aspirations of the Indian nation and its people.

As scholars have pointed out, by emphasising the communally divided nature of Indian society as an inescapable condition, the colonial state would indefinitely defer or refuse to accept that the Indian people had arrived at a point where they were capable of self-rule.[15] Therefore, Indian nationalists had to force the issue in the struggle for independence and pitch for a new Constitution that would give voice to the will of the Indian people understood as a community of free and equal citizens.[16]

When drafting the new Constitution, however, Indian nationalists could not escape confronting the colonial Constitution they had inherited and the identities and interests it had lodged in Indian society. This inherited model of constitutional organisation had, as already noted, produced for many decades a constitutional practice rooted in Indian social division. It was this colonially or imperially entrenched 'cleavage between different sections of the Indian nation' that those like Munshi sought to confront and rework.

However, faced with strongly entrenched minority rights of the colonial period, early debates of the Constituent Assembly were resigned to carrying forward a form of minority rights similar to that of the colonial state. In fact, in early deliberations, the Constituent Assembly even adopted a report by the Advisory Committee on Fundamental Rights granting minorities a set of rights similar to those they had hitherto enjoyed under the colonial state. The only significant difference was the case of separate electorates, which many minorities enjoyed in British India, but which were not included in the Advisory Committee's report.[17] Thus, even though free and equal citizenship in an undivided nation was asserted as a broader constitutional goal, there seemed to be few options to accommodate minorities outside the community-based system of rights and privileges that minorities enjoyed in British India.

Early efforts to organise the rights of minorities for the new Constitution anticipated the Muslim League would join the Constituent Assembly's proceedings and that British India would remain undivided. However, partition changed the political dynamic of the constitution-making process by removing the Muslim League as a dominant force in Indian politics. This turn of events vastly strengthened the Indian National Congress, allowing it to push towards a vision for national unity founded on citizenship quite like the position envisioned by Pant and other nationalist voices of the Assembly.[18] Even so, the new system was not a straightforward and sweeping abrogation of the colonial system but a complex reworking of those governmental frames through which the leadership of the Constituent Assembly ratified a revised proposal on minority rights which recommended 'that the system of reservation for minorities other than Scheduled Castes in Legislatures be abolished'.[19]

The proposal to abolish 'reservations for minorities' sought to reorganise allotments in legislatures, executive positions, as well as government jobs that minorities enjoyed in the colonial state. To that extent, this change was a significant reworking of the colonial framework on minority rights.[20] Under this new framework, the Depressed Classes would no longer be recognised as minorities but nonetheless be eligible for all the privileges of the erstwhile minorities. Other religious and linguistic groups would continue to be identified as minorities but would now be only entitled to a much more limited set of rights extending to the establishment and management of educational institutions as well as the protection of language, script and culture.[21]

This reorganisation of minority rights was staunchly opposed by groups within the Muslim and Sikh communities, the more influential of the minority groups in colonial India. However, as Sardar Vallabhbhai Patel would assert to the Assembly,

> it was no longer appropriate in the context of free India and of present conditions that there should be reservation of seats for Muslims, Christians, Sikhs or any other religious minority. Although the abolition of separate electorates had removed much of the poison from the body politic, the reservation of seats for religious communities, it was felt, did lead to a certain degree of separatism and was to that extent contrary to the conception of a secular democratic state.[22]

Thus, by emphasising the 'poison' and 'separatism' of the colonial model of minority rights, Patel sought to move towards a constitutional model that recognised India as a multicultural state but foregrounded national unity and minimised the sense of separation of minority communities from the national mainstream. But how then was it possible to justify the Scheduled Castes as a distinct legal category who could retain rights to reserved quotas in legislatures and in government jobs which they enjoyed in the colonial state?

Scheduled Castes or Depressed Classes were, as already noted, groups recognised as 'minorities' (though not granted a separate electorate) by the colonial state owing to systemic forms of caste-based discrimination that suffused Indian social relations. Further, the Poona Pact functioned as a constitutional settlement that constrained any significant modifications of the rights and privileges of the Scheduled Castes. Of equal importance, by the time of the drafting of the Constitution the Scheduled Castes were arguably one of the most important socio-political factions of Indian politics and whose demands could not be ignored. Thus, the force of their demands owed to their numbers in the population, the normative charge associated with the discrimination they suffered, as well as the historical settlement of their demands in the Poona Pact.

By contrast, the Assembly could much more easily fend off similar demands from other minority communities such as the Sikhs and Muslims, whose demands the house felt would contribute to deepening division and separatism. Even so, these considerations in Indian constitutional politics had to be constitutionalised in a form that would be consistent with the nationalist aims to secure a political community of free and equal citizens. This was constitutionally organised through what was shaping up as a constitutional vision to secure transformative social reform.[23] Accordingly, special privileges for the Scheduled Castes were justified and legitimised as constitutionally driven change necessary to alleviate the ills of caste society.

The language of social reform and transformation allowed the Constitution-makers to treat minorities and castes as distinct identities presenting separate and unique problems. That is, social transformation of the polity was the language through which the Constitution justified preferential treatment for caste groups without disturbing the commitment to common citizenship. In addition, the special rights granted to castes were seen as temporary.[24] Collectively, this meant that these rights did not seriously dent the idea of a universal citizenship, but merely functioned as preconditions for a future polity with full freedom and equality for all.

On the other hand, there was a greater degree of permanence envisaged for the rights granted to religious and linguistic groups that the new Constitution recognised as minorities. However, these rights were not regarded as establishing deep vested communal interests and as threatening the idea of national unity. Consequently, it was this transformative approach to Indian constitutionalism that permitted the grant of different sets of rights to Scheduled Castes and to (other) minorities and yet present this as a part of an integrated journey towards equal citizenship.

However, the mere aspiration to reject communal division would not by itself secure a free and equal 'people', or the transformation of the unjust social forms on whose name sovereign power was being claimed. Securing these aims would demand that constitutional practice draw on its understanding of the new Constitution to engender a 'people' in ways that disavowed the conceptualisations of India as a divided society. Accordingly, this chapter proceeds to examine this challenge by drawing on judicial practice as it has decided important questions on the rights of minorities in the Constitution of independent India.

Therefore, examining judicial practice, this chapter illustrates a majoritarian conception of the 'people' that fragments the Indian body politic into a largely nationally, axiomatically, and doctrinally, organised Hindu majority set and entrenched against assorted minority communities. In turn, it will be argued that this conception of the Indian people re-inserts a communal representation of the people or the body politic that the Constitution-framers attempted to displace. It is this imagination of minority rights, especially the rights of religious minorities, that must now be examined.

Minority Rights in the Constitution of Independent India

Reframing the colonial framework on minority rights, the Constitution of independent India attempted to recast and represent the Indian people as a community of free citizens subject equally to the rule of law. Against that background, this section examines the newly formed contours of minority rights and the extent to which its design and practice have been able to roll back the colonial and communally divided representation of minority rights.

Outlines of the Constitutional Framework

The Indian Constitution as it currently stands grants rights to religious and linguistic minorities to protect their religious, cultural and linguistic traditions as well as the right to establish and operate educational institutions. These rights are granted to minorities in Articles 29 and 30 of the Constitution in addition to the fundamental rights to equality and freedom that they enjoy as citizens. Accordingly, Article 29(1) grants '*any section of citizens* ... having a distinct language, script or culture of its own ... the right to conserve the same' (emphasis added) and Article 30 grants 'minorities', whether based on religion or language, the right to establish and administer educational institutions of their choice. As the phrasing of these provisions reveal, there is an important difference between these articles, with only Article 30 mentioning the word 'minority'. However, as part of the fundamental rights chapter of the Constitution titled 'Cultural and Educational Rights', they are presumably closely tied to each other in their broad object and purpose.

In early drafts of these constitutional provisions, the right granted in Article 29 to conserve language, script or culture was also envisaged exclusively for minorities.[25] However, the eventual shape taken by Article 29 made it applicable to all citizens and not minorities alone as part of the effort to pull back from the extensive political rights granted to minorities in colonial India. Speaking in the Constituent Assembly on the draft version of Article 29, B. R. Ambedkar explained that the purpose behind this phrasing was a more inclusive approach to the term 'minority' than that associated with the term in colonial state practice. Thus, as he stated in the Assembly,

> *the term minority was used therein not in the technical sense of the word 'minority' as we have been accustomed to use it for the purpose of certain political safeguards,* such as representation in the Legislature, representation in the service and so on. The word is ... also used to cover minorities which are not minorities in the technical sense, but which are nonetheless minorities in the cultural and linguistic sense. That is the reason why we dropped the word 'minority' because we felt that the word might be interpreted in the narrow sense of the term when the intention of this House ... was to use the word 'Minority' in a much wider sense so as to give cultural protection to those who were technically not minorities but minorities nonetheless.[26] (Emphasis added)

Despite the family resemblances that Ambedkar sought to draw between 'minorities' in Articles 29 and 30, adjudicatory practice has drawn out clear distinctions between these two provisions. It has been emphasised that only Article 30 refers to 'minorities' and that only minorities identified under that provision would be permitted the right to establish and administer educational institutions. Further, judicial decisions have also held that the right of minorities to run educational institutions would not be restricted by Article 29 to impart instruction only in matters relating to language, script or culture.[27] In addition, even if Article 29 and other provisions of the Constitution (like Article 26[a][28] and Article 19[1][g][29]) could be read as granting similar rights to all individuals and groups, constitutional adjudication has treated Article 30 as a special right granting minorities greater autonomy over their educational institutions.

Perceptive scholarship has noted that the tendency of the courts to treat minority educational institutions on a special footing and grant them greater administrative autonomy has produced a scramble by different groups such as Jains, Lingayats and the Ramakrishna Mission, groups who would not ordinarily be recognised as minorities, to present themselves as minorities.[30] Arguably, from the point of view of the Constitution's liberal ambitions, this special rights approach is less preferable than one that views minority rights as enjoyed equally with all others who choose to exercise the privilege to establish and administer educational institutions. That is, even as minorities ought to have rights to their educational institutions, it is unclear why this right should be their exclusive privilege and denied to other groups who seek to provide education as a public good. However, the task of arriving at normatively preferred or correct interpretations of the Constitution is not the task that guides the efforts of this book. On the contrary, as in previous chapters, the following sections only seek to examine the conceptual contours of constitutional practice and the manner in which it represents the Indian people. Thus, following the manner in which minority rights have been understood as special entitlements, the following sections demonstrate the manner in which the identification of minorities has communally inflected the character of the Indian people.

Courts identifying minorities for the purposes of Article 30 have offered different answers to the problem across different cases. But even in examining judicial answers relating to minority identity, it is important to note that these responses have not been the principal problem that courts have grappled with in resolving interpretative challenges regarding Articles 29 and 30. That is, most of the questions regarding the identification and delimitation of minority rights have arisen in the context of disputes over the interpretation of the right to 'establish and administer educational institutions' as guaranteed under Article 30. In particular, they have pertained to the manner in which the rights of minority institutions under Article 30, especially those receiving state aid, are to be balanced against the general public interest to ensure other constitutional values like the freedom to impart education, as also non-discrimination, and equal access to quality education.[31] Therefore, with their eye on balancing these values, a bulk of the judicial attention has often just presumed the identity of minority groups while demarcating the extent to which they can autonomously manage their educational institutions,[32] free from state oversight.

In balancing these constitutional values, courts have generally taken the position that protecting the rights granted to minorities in Article 30 only permits minimal state interference to ensure basic educational quality and that educational institutions are not completely unavailable to the general public.[33] Thus, in performing this balancing act, courts have held regulatory intervention to promote efficiency of instruction, discipline, health, sanitation, morality and public order or to maintain academic standards, infrastructure and general administrative standards to be permissible.[34] On the other hand, issues pertaining to admitting students, fee structures, internal governance, faculty appointments, disciplinary action, and so on, were held to be matters for internal institutional resolution.[35] Therefore, it is through balancing these competing issues that a majority of the questions regarding the rights of minorities in Article 30 have been demarcated and made viable.

The changing contours of the political economy of education as well as those of affirmative action have made this task of balancing contending interests and values particularly complex and challenging. Thus, to take an example, the *Pramati* decision[36] illustrates how courts had to contend with the right of minority institutions to autonomously administer their institutions when set against the Right of Children to Free and Compulsory Education Act, 2009 (hereinafter Compulsory Education Act), which was passed to implement the fundamental right to education as laid out in Article 21A of the Constitution. The former statute set out basic standards that institutions of primary education had to meet. In addition, Section 12(1)(c) of the Compulsory Education Act also mandated that 25 per cent of the seats in unaided private schools be allotted and reserved for children from backward and economically disadvantaged sections of society. *Pramati* is significant as it relieves all minority institutions from abiding by the limits specified by the Compulsory Education Act even when they receive aid from governments.

It could be argued that this conclusion has permitted the court to excessively veer towards recognising the right of minority communities to autonomously manage their educational institutions.[37] The *Pramati* decision does not of course fully capture the long arc of judicial practice resolving tensions between state interests when intervening in education in public interest and the rights of minorities to manage their institutions with a measure of autonomy. Nonetheless, it does reveal the contending values and interests that must be balanced and what is at stake in the protection of minority rights in a country where education is a relatively scarce and much valued public good.[38]

Against the background of this balancing act, the task of identifying a minority group has often taken backstage. Even so, to the extent that courts have been drawn into resolving questions of minority identity, they have considered questions such as whether a minority community is to be identified or determined the level of the Indian union as a whole or at the level of the federating state;[39] whether the minority institution was indeed instituted by minorities for the service of a minority community; and whether educational institutions claiming to be set up by minorities were in fact catering to and serving the educational needs of minority students.[40] Appropriate responses to such questions have for the most part been skeletal and cursory and do not by themselves reveal the criteria and the political sociology against which a minority is demarcated and therefore eligible to the rights granted by Article 30. Further, as there is no fixed constitutional definition of a minority, resolving questions regarding the criteria identifying minorities is best made through an examination of judicial decisions where minorities have made claims to be recognised as such and the challenges that courts have faced in granting or refusing such demands.

Article 30 grants rights to both religious and linguistic minorities. However, as this book emphasises the influence of religion on the making of Indian constitutional identity, the present examination of minority rights will also emphasise the identification of religious over linguistic minorities. This emphasis would not be out of place in examining the operation of Article 30, as a bulk of the adjudicatory practice on this provision is also devoted to resolving disputes about religious minorities as opposed to linguistic minorities.[41] As previously noted, this is almost certainly tied to the constitution of the colonial state and the central place it accorded to the representation of religious minorities such as the Muslims and the Sikhs. Therefore, it is through examination of the adjudicatory challenges of identifying religious minorities that this chapter will tease out the continuing presence of irreconcilable communal division, the most significant marker of constitutional identity in the Colonial Constitution.

Two Ways of Framing Minority Rights

As noted earlier in this chapter, minority rights in the contemporary Constitution carries only vestigial remains of the colonial approach to minorities and their rights. Thus, even in recognising the significance of minority rights for the new Constitution, the Constitution-makers made considerable efforts to ensure that these rights would not reproduce a communal account of the Indian people. It is against this background that the communal identification of religious minorities in adjudicatory practice is made salient.

As delimiting minority identity in constitutional adjudication often leaves implicit its conceptual assumptions, it is useful to make explicit these assumptions as frames that have cast minority identity along two analytically distinct paths. The first of these frames religious minorities by emphasising their distinctness from the national mainstream or a majority. Necessarily this frame is particularly attentive to the identity of the nation itself from which a minority is distinct. In the historical sweep of the Indian state this national identity, insofar as it is tied to religion, has been identified with a doctrinally and axiomatically demarcated 'Hindu' religion.[42] As an aspect of the Indian people, this nationally demarcated Hindu identity and related minority identities are well described by the Nehru Report of 1928 in the following manner:

> *The communal problem in India is essentially the Hindu-Muslim problem.* Other communities have however latterly taken up an aggressive attitude and have demanded special rights and privileges. The Sikhs in the Punjab are an important and well-knit community which cannot be ignored. Amongst the Hindus themselves there is occasional friction especially in the south, between non-Brahmans and Brahmans. But essentially the problem is how to adjust the differences between Hindus and Muslims.[43] (Emphasis added)

This account of the 'communal problem' seemingly reproduces the political sociology of the colonial state that viewed India as divided among its various communities. However, there is a subtle difference in that the Nehru Report re-presents the demands for recognition from various social groups as being principally reducible to 'the differences between Hindus and Muslims'. In other words, the colonial framework of social division is finely re-organised by foregrounding a Hindu majority against which other minorities take shape and of whom the Muslims are arguably the most important. Though the partition of British India weakened the pre-eminence of Muslims as the most significant minority community of India, the broader picture of Indian national identity defined against the background of a Hindu religious majority continued to remain important to understand, describe and demarcate religious identity. Consequently, in this framework, religious minorities came to be defined as identity groups distinct from what was presumably a doctrinally demarcated and national majority of Hindus.

It is important to note that understanding political community in India against the background of a Hindu majority is not merely a matter of sociological description. That is, casting political community in terms of a Hindu majority and other assorted minorities is as much part of a conceptual framework that constitutional institutions have deployed to speak of the Indian people. In other words, terms like 'Hindu' and 'Muslim' make salient the way local traditions have been cast and recast as constituent elements of the Indian body politic or its people.

The religious identities of the Indian people have been identified in other ways as well. Therefore, implicitly pushing against a nationally articulated Hindu majority is a second analytical frame that casts the Indian people, and by extension minorities, as part of a broader social plurality. This section terms this perspective on political community and on minorities as the account of plurality describing minorities.

In constitutional adjudication, plural accounts describing minorities can be drawn out of constitutional reasoning that engages and foregrounds Indian social diversity. These could be attempts by courts to amplify self-descriptions of diverse social groups or, alternatively, numerical descriptions of social groups constituting less than half the population of a state as eligible to be recognised as minorities.[44] *Prima facie*, these are entirely reasonable ways of approaching minorities as the Indian social milieu is intuitively associated with enormous plurality. However, to the extent that such claims permit any group within the 'Hindu' majority to claim that they also be recognised as a minority, this framework could dismember the earlier perspective or framework that casts 'Hindus' to be the religious majority of India. To that extent, even as it functions as a socially plausible form of identifying community, it has also run up against the more hegemonic view that sees religious minorities in India as defined against a Hindu majority. Consequently, illustrating the salience of a nationally organised Hindu identity, the following sections will demonstrate the manner in which the adjudication of minority rights has reinforced a majoritarian and communal conception of the Indian people.

The Majoritarian Background of Minority Rights

At the intersection of frames defining minority identities, Hindu groups claiming to be minorities have presented the most pressing challenge for the identification of religious minorities. That is, they challenge the common-sense proposition that the 'Hindus' constitute the religious majority among the Indian people. In challenging and testing the limits of this proposition, these groups often foreground plural forms of identification that are commonplace in Indian society. The intuitive resonance of these plural arguments have caused considerable problems for courts seeking to defend the demarcation of the political community into a Hindu majority and minorities and understood in relation to a Hindu majority. This challenge has brought contending frames about minority rights and political community to a head which are explored in the following cases.

In *Bramchari Sidheswar Bhai v. State of West Bengal*,[45] decided in 1995, the Ramakrishna Mission Residential College found itself in conflict with the revised policies of the Government of West Bengal regarding the college's management. The college was established by the Ramakrishna Mission in 1960 at the request of the West Bengal state government and was partially funded by both the central and the state governments. The Ramakrishna Mission is a religious organisation devoted to the teachings of the spiritual seer Sri Ramakrishna Paramhansa, and when the college was established the state government exempted it from government rules pertaining to the governance of academic institutions. However, subsequent government action revoked such exemptions, which the college challenged claiming theirs was a minority religious institution under Article 30, and thus enjoyed special rights to administer the college autonomously and free of government interference as protected by Article 30.

The Ramakrishna Mission is commonly believed to be part of a broader Hindu community. But in advancing their claim to be a minority community, the Ramakrishna Mission argued that they constituted a world religion and were not simply a parochial sect within Hinduism. They noted that Ramakrishna Paramhansa, their spiritual founder, 'practiced various religions including Islam and realized the truth underlying these religions ... That all religions are true ... that all religions are only different paths leading to the same goal'.[46] Along these lines, the Mission argued that it was distinctive in that it allowed members and followers to retain their identity as a Christian, Muslim, Jew, Hindu and such like while also simultaneously being members of the Mission.

This distinction echoes and draws on the very influential *Swaminarayan* case where also the Indian Supreme Court had to confront a form of Hindu pantheism that the Swaminarayan community, an influential Vaishnava sect, deployed to argue that they did not constitute any part of a doctrinally and axiomatically founded Hindu religion.[47] Drawing on this account of their tradition, the Ramakrishnas, as also the Swaminarayans, argued that they were a distinct religious group, in this case a minority, and not simply a strand within the Hindu majority.

The argument of the Ramakrishna Mission was accepted by the High Court at Kolkata, though on appeal the Indian Supreme Court overturned the High Court decision holding that the Ramakrishna Mission could not credibly claim to place itself apart from the broader Hindu community. Further, since most Indians identified as affiliated to the Hindu community, the Ramakrishna Mission could not claim minority status under Article 30.

Across both the *Ramakrishna* and *Swaminarayan* cases it was not clear how their traditions could be cast as distinct from the Hindu 'religion' understood doctrinally and axiomatically. To answer this question the Indian Supreme Court in both these cases dwelt in great length on an insoluble distinction between doctrinal and plural descriptions of the Hindu religion.

Thus, to excerpt from the Swaminarayan decision, the court drew on intuitive plural sociologies about the Hindu religion to assert that the Hindu religion

> does not claim any one prophet; it does not worship any one God; it does not subscribe to any one dogma; it does not believe in any one philosophic concept; it does not follow any one set of religious rites or performances; in fact, it does not appear to satisfy the narrow traditional features of any religion or creed. It may broadly be described as a way of life and nothing more.[48]

On the other hand, the court also cast a doctrinal net over the Hindu religion to declare that

> [b]eneath the diversity of philosophic thoughts, concepts and ideas expressed by Hindu philosophers ... lie certain broad concepts which can be treated as basic. The first amongst these basic concepts is the acceptance of the Veda as the highest authority in religious and philosophic matters.[49]

Across both these cases, the court drew on this latter account of the Hindu religion to argue that there was an axiomatic doctrinal core to the Hindu religion that pulled together its deep diversity into one composite and scripturally rooted community.

In other words, the court in both decisions draped an overarching axiomatic and doctrinal frame on Hindu belief and practice and held that the Swaminarayans and the Ramakrishna Mission were part of this conception of the Hindu community. This opinion stood at odds with the self-presentation of these groups as distinct communities in a manner entirely consistent with India's millennial traditions of pluralism and diversity. Nonetheless, across both these cases, the court simply incorporated and absorbed the plural perspective as a superstitious accretion over Hindu identity and doctrine.

The *Swaminarayan* case was a case on religious freedom and therefore it could be argued that questions relating to the identification of the body politic did not arise in that case. However, in the *Ramakrishna* case, the edging out of plural accounts of the Indian people is far more obviously tied to and set against the imagination of the body politic understood as defined by a Hindu majority. Even so, there are no clear reasons that the court advances on why it was compelled to affirm a doctrinal account of the Hindu traditions over a civilisational characterisation. That is, the court did not marshal any argument to disarm the intuitive sociological appeal of the plural accounts of Hindu religiosity. On the contrary, the court simply asserts that the doctrinal and axiomatic account of the Hindu religion trumps a plural characterisation of the Hindu traditions.

By contrast, it is useful to examine a later decision of the court in *Bal Patil & Anr. v. Union of India*,[50] which addresses the plural approach to Hindu religious identity and the anxieties it produces for the conceptualisation of the nation or the people – a problem that has played and continues to play an important role in making and sustaining Indian constitutional identity. In the *Bal Patil* case, the Supreme Court dismissed a petition of the Jain community arguing that the central government ought to have declared them a minority under the Minorities Commission Act, 1992. This law gave statutory footing to the National Commission for Minorities which was a body that had been in existence since 1978. The functions of the commission included making recommendations for the welfare of minorities, including the safeguarding and protection of their constitutional rights. However, the power to declare a community to be a minority under the statute was vested not in the commission but in the central government. Accordingly, the government declared Muslims, Sikhs, Christians, Parsis and Buddhists as minorities, but left the

Jains out of this list. The Jains then petitioned the Supreme Court to direct the government to include them in the list of minorities. This is important as it has a bearing on the identification and recognition of minorities who in turn are entitled to the privileges under Article 30, which must have been a driver of the Jain petition.

Addressing the Jain petition, the court held that the power to declare a minority was vested in the central government and that it was inappropriate for the court to second-guess this exercise of executive discretion. Nevertheless, a significant portion of the court's opinion examined possible justifications for the government's exclusion of the Jains. It is this *obiter dicta* supporting the government's decision that permits this section to take a lens to the tense relationship between demarcating the Indian people based on social diversity and plurality, and the backdrop of a doctrinally and axiomatically founded Hindu community.

Insofar as their status as minorities is concerned, the Jains have always been a hard case. They have sometimes been identified as being part of the broader Hindu community,[51] and at other times they have been identified to be a distinct community.[52] In any event, despite an adverse decision from the court, the Jains would eventually succeed in pressing the government to have themselves declared a minority community under the Minorities Commission Act in early 2014. Nonetheless, in confronting this ambiguous status of the Jains, Justice Dharmadhikari throws light on the difficulty that the Jains posed to delineating and defending a unified Indian nation and its people. According to him, 'Hindu society ... is itself divided into various minority groups ... In a caste-ridden Indian society, no section or distinct group of people can claim to be in a majority. *All are minorities among the Hindus*[53] (emphasis added). Consequently, he exhorted the government not to recognise minorities in ways that encouraged groups like the Jains to adopt what he called a 'minority sentiment'. Doing so would fragment the conceptualisation of political community on which constitutional identity in India was built.

Of course, Muslim assertion of a distinct minority identity would presumably not trouble Justice Dharmadhikari as much as claims made by groups like the Ramakrishna Mission, the Swaminarayans and, in this case, the Jains. When religion is the marker of Indian national identity, Muslims and certain other religious groups have more easily been recognised as distinct from the dominant strands of national culture and identity. But from Justice Dharmadhikari's vantage point, the Jains form part of the social spectrum that constitutes the (Hindu) majority that marked the religious identity of the Indian people. Consequently, any demand for minority status from groups along this spectrum would, in his opinion, fracture the nation's Hindu identity and its unifying political force. Therefore, it is in this manner that a doctrinally and axiomatically conceived Hindu community has fed into a national and potentially majoritarian identity against which minority identity has acquired salience and recognition.

The *Ramakrishna* and *Bal Patil* cases are not by any means exceptions as there have been other decisions advancing similar arguments on religion in Indian national and constitutional identity. Thus, in the *Arya Samaj Education Trust* case[54] the court argued that

> [t]he nation has to guard against all kinds of disruptions. There is a prevailing tendency in spiritual ambition which leading to diverse expositions is causing the coming into being of various religious denominations. Such denominations ought not to be allowed to prevail as religion should not be confounded as separate religions.[55]

However, expressing his complete disagreement with this manner of argument, H. M. Seervai argues that 'it is not for the court to cut down fundamental rights because the court thinks that national interests require that the Hindu religion should not include minorities based on religion.'[56] Seervai's assertion could be logically extended to support the claims of groups like the Ramakrishnas and the Jains. However, even as courts have not gone quite as far, decisions like that issued by the constitution bench judgment in the *TMA Pai* case seem to back away from casting minorities as groups understood against the background of a Hindu majority. In that decision, the court echoed judicial opinion that a minority could be any group that constituted less than half the population of any of India's federating states. That is, in making this pronouncement on the identification of minorities the court took a step away from the position that a nationally identified Hindu community constituted the religious majority that made up the Indian people. However, even as an extremely important decision that offers an alternative axis to characterise and identify minorities, it is unclear whether the conceptual span of this opinion is wide enough to accommodate arguments drawing on social plurality advanced by communities like the Ramakrishnas or the Jains.

The identification of minorities in decisions like *TMA Pai* was tied to the federating states of the Indian union. As the states are primarily organised on linguistic lines, it could be said that the case emphasises linguistic minorities as part of an institutional scheme that emphasises the plurality of the states.[57] That is, by pushing the level of determination of a minority to that of a federating unit, *TMA Pai* opens out a measure of recognition to a plurality of minorities, especially linguistic minorities as identified at the level of the states. In addition, this approach also removes the logically counterintuitive possibility of a community that is a minority at the level of the nation but a majority in the relevant state being declared a minority in that state. An example of this kind would be the case of Telegu speakers who are a majority in the Telegu-speaking states but a minority nationally, or Sikhs who are a religious majority in the state of Punjab but a minority nationally. In such situations, the court held that the forty-second amendment to the Constitution that moved education from being a state legislative subject to one on which the central government could also legislate did not come in the way of identifying minorities at the level of the state.

The *TMA Pai* decision clearly envisages an institutional scheme for the recognition of a plurality of linguistic minorities at the level of the states. Of more significance to this chapter, it has been held in other cases that religious groups also were to be treated on a par with linguistic groups. That is, religious minorities also were to be determined at the level of the relevant states. In one such case, this approach was adopted by the Supreme Court to educational institutions run by the Arya Samaji Hindus recognising them as minorities with respect to educational institutions they administered in the state of Punjab made up of a Sikh religious majority.[58] On the face of the matter, this approach acknowledges the importance of recognising the changing numerical dynamics of religious or linguistic groups as they vary across states. However, on closer scrutiny the *Arya Samaj* case also betrays a nationalist and even majoritarian background to identifying minorities, only that the frame of identifying a minority has shifted from a country-wide level to that of the federating state.

Shifting the level at which a minority is to be identified does permit some degree of recognition for plurality of identities. However, it also reveals a constraint in the *TMA Pai* type framework which is best explained by the manner in which state-level identification of minorities was unable to address the problem that the Arya Samaji community case posed. That is, that the Arya Samajis could only be identified within the framework of an axiomatically and doctrinally organised Hindu identity. Their late-nineteenth-century reforming tradition was of course premised on presenting and resituating the fragmented ritualist strands of Hindu practice as founded on what they took to be a unifying Vedic and pan-Hindu doctrine.[59] Nevertheless, and reading both the claims of the Arya Samajis as well as court itself against their grain, for all their significance as an important religious reform movement of the broader 'Hindu' tradition, the framework of pluralism could justifiably cast them as just another group in the background that makes up the plurality of Indian society. However, wedded to a majoritarian frame of identifying minorities, the court could only identify them as a Hindu minority in a Sikh Punjab. It must of course be emphasised that neither the court nor the Arya Samajis themselves entertained such argument about their distinctness within a broader civilisational pluralism. These arguments are therefore advanced merely to illustrate the limitations in merely altering the level at which a minority is identified as also to illustrate that the framework of pluralism could plausibly absorb the Arya Samajis as part of the pluralism that marks Indian society.

However, as with the Ramakrishnas and the Jains, the courts have been far more comfortable identifying religious minorities as groups that assume salience against a majority group constituting the body politic or the people as a whole. In most cases, Hindus have been identified as the majority against which religious minorities were recognised, though in exceptional instances like that of the Arya Samajis in the Punjab, even Hindus could be viewed as minorities. However, across all these instances it was an axiomatically organised majority identity that gave salience to religious minorities.

Thus, at the intersection of the alternative frames of defining minority rights identified by this chapter, nationally and pan-territorially demarcated majorities have formed the background against which minority religious identities have been determined in constitutional practice. This way of defining minority identity has of course been credibly challenged by groups such as the Ramakrishnas, the Jains, the Lingayats, and so on, all of whom have drawn on arguments from plurality to present themselves as minority communities. However, when faced with claims for recognition that draw on arguments from social and civilisational plurality, it has been more than likely that courts will entrench nationally and pan-territorially and axiomatically organised communal identities to characterise the background against which minority identity is represented. Therefore, it is in this respect that communally organised identities have shaped minority identities as also the broader identity of the Indian people. Consequently, it is on this note that this chapter draws its account on minority rights to a conclusion.

Conclusion

Pulling together its strands of discussion, this chapter has described the communal manner in which the Indian people have been organised: first, through the prism of division fashioned by the colonial state and, later, in the entrenched nationalist majoritarian frames that identified minorities in adjudicatory practice. Therefore, like in previous chapters, through a discussion on minority rights this chapter has sought to demonstrate the manner in which the colonial prism of minority rights continues to influence contemporary constitutional practice.

Lastly, the discussion on minority rights in this chapter has left unexamined the form in which the Constitution resolved the rights of the Depressed Classes or Scheduled Castes as it reorganised the frame of minority rights inherited from the colonial Constitution. As a minority in colonial India the Scheduled Castes were equally tied to the problem of a communal constituent imagination inherited from the colonial state and carried into the contemporary Constitution. Therefore, it is this aspect of the colonial resolution of minority rights that must now be examined. Accordingly, examining the determination of caste identity it will be argued that the resolution of the rights of caste groups is also tied to a nationally organised communal account of the Indian people.

Notes

1. For a detailed discussion on the idea of colonial trusteeship as well as the form in which they translated into the debates on the making of the government of India Acts of 1909, 1919 and 1935, see Coupland, *Report on the Constitutional Problem in India; S. V. Desika Char (ed.), Readings in the Constitutional History of India 1757–1947* (New Delhi: Oxford University Press, 1983); Uday Singh Mehta, *Liberalism and Empire: India in British Liberal Thought* (New Delhi: Oxford University Press 1999); Sufiya Pathan, 'A Historical and Theoretical Investigation into Communalism' (thesis submitted to Manipal University, 2009).
2. Coupland, *Report on the Constitutional Problem in India*, 18.
3. Thomas Babington Macaulay, 'Government of India', *Miscellaneous Writings and Speeches*, vol. 4 (Project Gutenberg, 2008), https://www.gutenberg.org/files/2170/2170-h/2170-h.htm, accessed 8 November 2022.
4. 'East India (Advisory and Legislative Councils, &c.). Vol. I. Proposals of the Government of India and Despatch of the Secretary of State' (1908), 2, http://gateway.proquest.com/openurl?url_ver=Z39.88-2004&res_dat=xri:hcpp&rft_dat=xri:hcpp:rec:1908-010247, accessed 24 April 2010.
5. For example, see Char, *Readings in the Constitutional History of India 1757–1947*. See also James Chiriyankandath, '"Democracy" under the Raj: Elections and Separate Representation in British India', *Journal of Commonwealth and Comparative Politics* 30, no. 1 (1992): 39.
6. Char, *Readings in the Constitutional History of India*, 431.
7. 'Report on Indian Constitutional Reform' (Calcutta: Superintendent Government of India Press, 1918), 149.

8. Chiriyankandath, "'Democracy" under the Raj'.
9. 'Report on Indian Constitutional Reform', 85.
10. For a more detailed account of the debates that preceded the 1909 and 1919 statutes and especially its representation of the Indian people as a collection of communally organised minorities, see Pathan, 'A Historical and Theoretical Investigation into Communalism', 249–304.
11. Hereinafter the term will be used interchangeably with 'Depressed Castes'. These groups were recognised as minorities earlier as well, but as minorities nominated by the government under the 1919 Act.
12. Char, *Readings in the Constitutional History of India*, 561–63. See also Rochana Bajpai, *Debating Difference: Group Rights and Liberal Democracy in India* (Oxford: Oxford University Press, 2011).
13. B. Shiva Rao, et al., *The Framing of India's Constitution*, vol. 2 (New Delhi: Indian Institute of Public Administration, 1966), 61.
14. For example, see Judith M. Brown, *Modern India: The Origins of an Asian Democracy* (Oxford: Oxford University Press, 1985).
15. For example, see Mehta, *Liberalism and Empire*; Dipesh Chakrabarthy, 'Postcoloniality and the Artifice of History: Who Speaks for "Indian" Pasts?' *Representations* 37 (Winter 1992): 1.
16. For example, see Chatterjee, *The Nation and Its Fragments*.
17. Part. XIV of the Draft Constitution of February 1948.
18. See Bajpai, *Debating Difference*; see also Iqbal Ansari, 'Minorities and the Politics of Constitution Making in India', in *Minority Identities and the Nation-State*, ed. D. Sheth and Gurpreet Mahajan, 111–23 (New Delhi: Oxford University Press, 1999).
19. *Constituent Assembly Debates: Official Report*, vol. 4 (New Delhi: Lok Sabha Secretariat, 1999), 601.
20. For a detailed account of this transition to the new Constitution, see Bajpai, *Debating Difference*.
21. See Articles 29 and 30.
22. B. Shiva Rao et al., *The Framing of India's Constitution*, vol. 4 (New Delhi: Indian Institute of Public Administration, 1966), 600.
23. See Granville Austin, *The Indian Constitution: Cornerstone of a Nation* (New Delhi: Oxford University Press, 1966); Uday Singh Mehta, 'Constitutionalism', in *The Oxford Companion to Politics in India*, ed. Niraja Gopal Jayal and Pratap Bhanu Mehta, 15–27 (New Delhi: Oxford University Press, 2010); Gautam Bhatia, *The Transformative Constitution: A Radical Biography in Nine Acts* (New Delhi: HarperCollins India, 2019).
24. *Constitution of India*, Article 334.
25. Rao et al., *The Framing of India's Constitution*, vol. 2, 208–09.

26. *Constituent Assembly Debates: Official Report*, vol. 7 (New Delhi: Lok Sabha Secretariat, 1999), 922–23.

27. *St. Xavier College v. State of Gujarat* AIR 1974 SC 1389.

28. The right of religious denominations to establish and maintain institutions for religious and charitable purposes.

29. The freedom of citizens to practise any profession, or to carry on any occupation, trade or business.

30. K. Vivek Reddy, 'Minority Educational Institutions', in *The Oxford Handbook of the Indian Constitution*, ed. Sujit Choudhry, Madhav Khosla and Pratap Bhanu Mehta, 921–942 (New Delhi: Oxford University Press, 2016), 931–32.

31. The general contours of equality and non-discrimination are detailed in Articles 14 and 15 of the Constitution but these values are also contained more pointedly in provisions such as in Article 29(2) which states that citizens shall not be denied admission to state run educational institutions and institutions receiving state support 'on grounds only of religion, race, caste or language'.

32. In this respect, it is perhaps also important to mention Article 30(2) which prevents the state from discriminating against educational institutions run by minority communities when disbursing grants-in-aid.

33. For the nuance of judicial reason on these questions, see Ajey Sangai, Akriti Gaur, Arghya Sengupta and Shruti Ambasht, 'Right to Education and Minority Rights: Towards a Fine Constitutional Balance' (New Delhi: Vidhi Centre for Legal Policy, 2016); Reddy, 'Minority Educational Institutions'.

34. *Rev. Sidhajbhai Sabhai and Ors. v State of Bombay*, [1963] 3 SCR 837; *TMA Pai v. State of Karnataka* (2002) 8 SCC 481; Sangai et al., 'Right to Education and Minority Rights'.

35. Sangai et al., 'Right to Education and Minority Rights'.

36. (2014) 8 SCC 1.

37. Sangai et al., 'Right to Education and Minority Rights'.

38. For example, see Rajeev Dhavan and Fali S Nariman, 'The Supreme Court and Group Life: Religious Freedom, Minority Groups and Disadvantaged Communities', in *Supreme but Not Infallible: Essays in Honour of the Supreme Court of India*, ed. B. N. Kirpal and Ashok Desai, 256–89 (New Delhi: Oxford University Press 2000); Sangai et al., 'Right to Education and Minority Rights'.

39. See *TMA Pai v. State of Karnataka* (2002) 8 SCC 481.

40. H. M. Seervai, *Constitutional Law of India*, vol. 2 (4th edn, Bombay: Universal Law Publishing – An imprint of LexisNexis, 2015).

41. Relatedly it is also interesting to note that in the drafting of Articles 29 and 30 in the Constituent Assembly, Muslim members tried to argue for the

recognition of Urdu speakers as a distinct minority group. This is illustrated in the interventions of members like Z. H. Lahiri, Maulana Hasrat Maohoni and Kazi Syed Karimuddin. *Constituent Assembly Debates: Official Report*, vol. 7, 891–930.

42. Chapters 1 and 2.
43. *The Nehru Report: An Anti-Separatist Manifesto* (New Delhi: Michiko & Panjathan, under the auspices of the Indian Institute of Applied Political Research, 1975), 27.
44. See *TMA Pai v. State of Karnataka* (2002) 8 SCC 481, 551–53.
45. MANU/SC/0413/1995.
46. MANU/SC/0413/1995, para 24.
47. *Sastri Yagnapurushdasji v. Muldas Bhudardas Vaishya* AIR 1966 SC 1119 (henceforth *Swaminarayan* case).
48. *Swaminarayan* case, 1128.
49. *Swaminarayan* case, 1130.
50. *Bal Patil & Anr. v. Union of India* MANU/SC/0472/2005.
51. For example, see Section 2 of the Hindu Marriage Act of 1955.
52. See Survepalli Radhakrishnan, *Indian Philosophy*, vol. 1 (London: George Allen and Unwin Ltd, 1948), 361.
53. *Bal Patil & Anr. v. Union of India*, para 34.
54. AIR 1976 Delhi 207.
55. AIR 1976 Delhi 219.
56. Seervai, *Constitutional Law of India*, vol. 2, 1330–31.
57. See *TMA Pai v. State of Karnataka* (2002) 8 SCC 481.
58. *D. A. V. College v. State of Punjab* 1971(2)SCC 269.
59. See Kenneth W Jones, *Socio-Religious Reform Movements in British India* (New Delhi: Cambridge University Press, 1994).

4

Sacralising Caste

The Hindu Resolution of Equal Citizenship

As observed in the previous chapter, the reorganisation of minority rights in independent India was the result of a new constitutional imagination justified as the transformation of Indian society. Reorganising the colonial government of 'minorities', the project of social transformation unfolded a forked path to recognise and incorporate minorities and Scheduled Castes into the Constitution of independent India. Both these newly recognised constitutional groups were envisaged as axes of identity facilitating a project for the social transformation of the Indian people understood as a liberal and secular community of free and equal citizens. However, as argued in the last chapter, despite the best laid intentions of the Constitution-makers, constitutional design and practice operated to reinforce and entrench communally ordered religious identities that demarcated the Indian people into majorities and minorities.

This chapter will show that the design and defence of the rights of the Scheduled Castes also suffer a similar problem. That is, caste injustice is constitutionally framed and resolved as a Hindu problem. Besides flying in the face of the fact that caste injustice in India is not restricted to any one communal group, the 'Hindu' resolution of caste also nationalises and entrenches caste in explicitly communal terms. This communal resolution of the problem of the Scheduled Castes has had ripple effects on related constitutional debates as well, especially on the rights of social groups the Constitution terms the 'Backward Classes'. Accordingly, elaborating the constitutional scheme pertaining to Scheduled Castes and the Backward Classes, this chapter spotlights the manner in which their rights are secured against the background of a communal and Hindu representation of the Indian people.

The Background

The Scheduled Castes, or the Depressed Classes as they were known in the colonial state, were drawn into Indian constitutional imagination as minorities.[1] Their inclusion in colonial legislatures as minorities was intended to represent the voice of social groups suffering from systemic forms of discrimination on account of caste society, most notably through the practice of untouchability. These social groups first found representation in colonial legislatures following the Government of India Act of 1919. However, unlike other important minorities such as the Muslims and the Sikhs, Depressed Class representatives were not drawn into colonial legislatures through separate or reserved electorates but by way of state nomination.[2] Even so, by the time of the Government of India Act of 1919, the issue of political recognition for Scheduled Castes on account of the injustice and discrimination they faced was well and truly part of the national political imagination. Accordingly, it is useful to start this chapter with a short outline of the emergence of caste as an important problem that would define Indian constitutional identity.

As a problem that demanded the reorganisation of Indian society, political representation and programmes in favour of the Depressed Classes were not always a preferred solution. For instance, resisting the reform of caste relations as part of the national programme of the Indian National Congress, Dadabhai Naoroji asks in 1886:

> [W]hat do any of us know of the internal home life, of the customs, traditions, feelings, prejudices of any class but our own? *How could a ... cosmopolitan gathering like this, discuss to any purpose the reform needed in any one class?* ... A National Congress must confine itself to questions in which the entire nation has a direct participation, and it must leave the adjustment of social reforms and other class questions to class Congresses.[3] (Emphasis added)

However, by the early part of the twentieth century, the reform of caste and caste relations was no longer an aspect of caste autonomy as it was increasingly regarded as an obstacle to national development and national consciousness.[4] As a sign of this broadly changing approach on the matter, it is useful to note the Congress resolution of 1917 urging the people of India to take note of the 'necessity, justice and righteousness of removing all disabilities imposed by custom upon the Depressed Classes the disabilities being of a most vexatious and oppressive character, subjecting those classes to considerable hardship and inconvenience'.[5]

In his defining work on the regulation of caste in modern India, Marc Galanter notes this change while pointing to the role played by the colonial government in nationalising the challenge of reforming the inequities of caste society.[6] The nationalisation of caste and its incorporation into the conceptualisations of the Indian people is a multilayered story but most centrally tied to the rise of ethnographic practices of the colonial government, primarily the census, that identified and recognised caste as a key axis of Indian social organisation in the latter half of the nineteenth century.[7] With this development, caste joined categories like religion as social phenomena through which the diversity of Indian society was to be understood, regulated and governed. Thus, as the ethnographic survey of India states in 1901, a well-arranged record of the castes and tribes of India was important as 'a record of the customs of the people is as necessary an incident of good administration as a cadastral survey of the land and a record of the rights of its tenants'.[8]

However, in addition to administrative motivations, quite like religion, caste was also envisaged as an axis along which the Indian people could be understood and represented in politics. Nicholas Dirks illustrates this aspect of caste by drawing on the census commissioner Herbert Risley to show that at the cusp of the twentieth century caste had come to be understood to be a 'kind of civil society for the colonial state'.[9] Collectively this political and administrative approach to caste evoked responses from Indian society in the form of caste-based organisations that took shape in various parts of the country. However, despite the crucial role that caste came to play in the constitutional politics of early-twentieth-century India, it was not settled how castes groups were to be inserted into the political institutions of British India.

Unlike Muslims, who were recognised as a religious minority group requiring special representation by the Indian Councils Act of 1909, no similar protection was granted to caste groups on an all-India basis until much later after the passage of the Government of India Act of 1919. However, as caste increasingly became an axis for political representation there was considerable anxiety about how it would be viewed as a constituent element of Indian society. As an aspect of Indian society Herbert Risley's reflections from the Indian census characterises caste in India as

[a] congenital instinct, an all-pervading principle of attraction and repulsion entering into and shaping every relation of life. For Hindus caste is bound up

with their religion, and its observance is enforced by the authority of the priests; its influence is conspicuous in the social usages of most Indian Muhammadans; and it extends even to the relatively small communities of Christians. Thus, it forms the cement that holds together the myriad units of Indian society.[10]

This account of caste clearly marks it out as the social glue that held all communities in Indian society in its grasp though with different valence for different communities.

It is this pervasiveness of caste that permitted Muslim representatives to credibly argue at the turn of the twentieth century that Depressed Classes subject to the injustices of caste society be treated as an independent social group for political representation.[11] This demand was undoubtedly tied to the new scramble for power in the constitutional institutions of colonial India between groups such as the Congress and the Muslim League in the first half of the twentieth century. But even so, it was not implausible to view the Depressed Classes as a *sui generis* group identifiable by the ubiquity of caste in Indian society. However, the depressed groups eventually came to be identified in British government as largely made up of Hindu untouchables. This chapter will argue that this identification of the untouchables flies in the face of evidence about caste, but to do so it is important to first sketch a brief account of the governmental recognition of the Depressed Castes solely as the excluded among Hindus.

Drawing on the possibilities offered by colonial institutions, the earliest political mobilisation of caste groups was made by those groups who put together an anti-Brahmin politics in provinces such as Madras and Bombay.[12] These non-Brahmin backward castes were an amorphous group fighting against the Brahmin monopoly of public life in colonial India and were largely understood to be at the lowest rungs of India's caste hierarchy. In some instances, they were understood to include the Depressed Classes and at other instances the Backward Classes were understood to include a group of castes a rung above the untouchable Depressed Classes. It was in response to the demands of these groups that the colonial government reserved places for them in jobs, educational institutions and in legislative bodies. Eventually the identity of the Depressed Classes as well as the institutional framework that addressed their concerns grew to be distinct from the way the backward castes and classes were identified and engaged and drawn into the colonial government. Even so, it was against this broader background that Depressed Classes were first nominated and drawn into the institutional framework of the colonial government.[13]

Depressed Classes were first nominated to colonial legislatures within the framework of the 1919 Act. However, it was only with the next round of constitutional change leading up to the Government of India Act of 1935 that there was a move to significantly increase the representation of the Depressed Classes in colonial legislatures. This increase was a result of protracted negotiations that began with the report of the Indian Statutory Commission and culminated in the Poona Pact. Though there were many twists and turns in these negotiations, the sticking point resolved at Poona was the infamous proposal called the 'communal award'. This proposal mooted by the British government recommended that the Depressed Classes be recognised as a minority in their own right and granted a separate electorate on grounds of the disability they suffered because of untouchability.[14]

As well known, M. K. Gandhi, who was vehemently opposed to separate electorates for the Depressed Classes, took to a hunger strike to wrest the Poona Pact from an unwilling B. R. Ambedkar, who had come to advocate separate electorates for the untouchables. Prior to the pact, discussing the proposals of the Indian Statutory Commission at the Round Table Conference in London, Gandhi opposed the communal award expressing his belief that untouchability was a blot to be removed through the reform of 'Hindu' society.[15] Gandhi could envisage a separate social identity for communities such as the Muslims and Sikhs to remain even in perpetuity but baulked at the thought that untouchables should be treated similarly. On the other hand, to Ambedkar the issue was simply about political rights for one-fifth of the population of British India who were isolated from the broader society and invidiously treated as untouchables. He also recognised like Gandhi that the problem of the Depressed Classes was rooted in the social problem of untouchability, but precisely for that reason he felt that the solution had to be 'political' – through the transfer of real electoral and political power to all untouchables as a distinct community.[16]

Thus, the stalemate unlocked by the Poona Pact advanced two different perspectives to the challenge that caste posed to the Indian people. To Gandhi, caste was a malignant and unjust accretion on Hindu society. Consequently, despite Gandhi's pantheism in understanding Hindu religiosity, resolving the challenge of caste injustice was not envisaged as a problem that could encompass other social groups such as Muslims, Christians or Buddhists whose social practices also displayed the inequities of caste society. By contrast, even as Ambedkar on occasion characterised caste society, and especially untouchability, as an organising principle of a scripturally and axiomatically organised 'Hindu' society, he sought to confront the inequities that it foregrounded as a secular and perhaps neutral political problem for the polity as a whole.

Ambedkar's hopes for a secular resolution of the caste problem were betrayed by the Poona Pact which did not recognise a separate political identity for the Depressed Classes.[17] Further, even as Ambedkar sought to present caste as a broader political problem, the confrontation over the communal award did not fundamentally challenge popular characterisation of caste as a Hindu issue. Therefore, it was as a Hindu problem that the settlement embodied in the Poona Pact was passed onto the Constitution-makers of independent India as they were reworking the system of minority rights in the Government of India Act of 1935. However, this raised the question of the way an avowedly secular republic could be seen as the custodian of Hindu religious and social reform.

That is, the Assembly had to resolve the problem of whether caste was the parochial problem of the Hindu community alone. Or whether it was a broader social problem that suffused the body politic at large. Accordingly, it is the form in which these questions were resolved by the Constitution of independent India that must now be examined.

Resolving the Caste Problem for the New Constitution

The Indian Constitution was designed, as already noted, to ameliorate the social condition of the Scheduled Castes, especially their disabilities stemming from untouchability. These constitutional ends were secured through a range of constitutional provisions that ensured representation of the Scheduled Castes in legislatures as well as provisions that sought to ensure the protection of their interests.

The most generally framed of these constitutional provisions is Article 14 of the Constitution, which requires the state to treat all citizens equally irrespective of caste, class and gender. However, precisely because of the inequities of deep-rooted social practices such as untouchability, it was also recognised that generally framed provisions would be inadequate to further the Constitution's broader vision for the transformation of Indian society.

Thus, the Constitution also included a set of provisions actively oriented towards the reorganisation of Indian social relations, especially those bearing on caste practice. In the Fundamental Rights chapter of the Constitution these provisions include: Article 15(2), which disallows the government or private persons from discriminating on the basis of caste in public places; Article 15(4), permitting governments to make positive discrimination measures for the Scheduled Castes, Scheduled Tribes and Other Backward Classes;[18] Article 15(5), permitting positive discrimination measures regarding admission to both government and even private educational institutions; Article 16(4), enabling compensatory discrimination in government jobs for Backward Classes of citizens; Article 17, abolishing untouchability; Article 23, abolishing forced labour of any kind; and Article 25(2), which, as discussed in Chapter 1, has permitted the state to make social reform and temple entry provisions for groups such as the Scheduled Castes. Besides these rights enumerated in the Fundamental Rights chapter of the Constitution, the Scheduled Castes are also allotted reserved seats in parliament and in the provincial state legislatures through Articles 330 and 332. Though these reservations were initially granted for a period of ten years, they have been repeatedly extended by parliament right up to the present day. In addition, Article 338 establishes the National Commission for the Scheduled Castes and Scheduled Tribes, which is a standing body that monitors and advises the government on the various rights and schemes for the benefit of the Scheduled Castes and Tribes. Lastly, it is perhaps also possible to view the entire scheme of rights for the Scheduled Castes as being guided by Article 46, a directive principle of the Constitution requiring the state to protect the interests of Scheduled Castes among other weaker sections.

This elaborate framework for the Scheduled Castes marks out the substantive concerns of the Indian state as it specifically bears on the problem of caste. The operation of these provisions forms an important part of Indian constitutional law addressing caste discrimination and the equal rights of citizens. However, this chapter, like the book as a whole, will gloss over this normative scheme envisaged for the Scheduled Castes and highlight instead the identification of Scheduled Castes as subjects of this scheme of transformative justice. In examining this question, this chapter is particularly concerned with the question of whether the social programme for Scheduled Castes in the Constitution continues to be identified, as in the colonial Constitution, with the reform of Hindu society. Or alternatively, would the Constitution be able to formulate the problem of caste in a less parochial fashion?

A cursory examination of the debates in the Constituent Assembly suggests that the Constitution-makers were unable to get past the contours of the colonial Constitution that, for the most part, defined the problem of caste inequity as an aberration in Hindu society. Thus, in an early debate on minority rights K. M. Munshi identified the challenge of untouchability and of accommodating the untouchables in the new constitutional politics by arguing that so far as the Scheduled Castes are concerned, they are not minorities in the strict meaning of the term; that the Harijans are part and parcel of Hindu community, and the safeguards are given to them to protect their rights only till they are completely absorbed in the Hindu Community.

...The distinction between Hindu Community other than Scheduled Castes and the Scheduled Castes is the barrier of untouchability. Now, by the Fundamental Rights which we have accepted, untouchability is prohibited by law and its practice is made a criminal offence under the law of the Federation. We have also accepted in the Fundamental Rights that no public place should be prohibited to anyone by reason of his birth. So far as the Federation is concerned, we have removed the artificial barrier between one section of the Hindu Community and the other[19]

In Munshi's account, untouchability is defined as a problem of the Hindus, and the constitutional bond is itself viewed as an act of Hindu redemption and as the removal of barriers between Hindu communities. As a Congress leader of note, Munshi was no outlier in the Constituent Assembly. Even a towering Congress figure like Sardar Vallabhbhai Patel made a rather similar statement when intervening in a Constituent Assembly debate considering the inclusion of some sections of the Sikh community in the list of Scheduled Castes. Expressing dismay at the Sikh demand, Patel stated that

> it was against our conviction to recognise a separate Sikh caste as untouchables or Scheduled Castes, because untouchability is not recognised in the Sikh religion. A Scheduled Caste Sikh community has never been in the past recognised.[20]
> (Emphasis added)

Though Patel acceded to the Sikh demands, his comments reveal the reasons behind his conviction that, unlike Hindu groups, the Sikh demands were not legitimate. This was because untouchability was not recognised in the Sikh religious canon or doctrine. By implication, the Sikhs could not legitimately claim inclusion of the backward sections of their community in the list of Scheduled Castes. However, Sardar Hukam Singh, whose statements in the Constituent Assembly prompted Patel's intervention, saw the problem of identification of the Scheduled Castes very differently and as simply involving the identification of groups suffering from the same disabilities and social practices.[21]

The point of view asserted by those like Hukam Singh to argue that the Scheduled Castes were merely those who suffered from a similar set of disabilities or social practices met with considerable resistance from those who understood caste to be a Hindu religious phenomenon. As with all contests over ideas, the contending positions over the nature of caste disability was not merely an intellectual difference over the nature of a concept but also one that related to material interests of different social groups. These included the fears that recognition of non-Hindu groups as Scheduled Castes would facilitate conversion to religions like Christianity,[22] or even the concerns of existing groups of Scheduled Castes, who feared dilution of existing privileges should the identification of Scheduled Castes be expanded to include non-'Hindu' groups.[23] It is beyond the scope of this chapter to examine these layers of material interests as they have diverged on the issue of identifying Scheduled Castes in Indian constitutional politics. However, drawing on Marc Galanter it is helpful to spotlight and conceptually clarify the distinctions at stake in the exchange between those such as Sardar Hukam Singh, on the one hand, and others such as Munshi and Patel, on the other, whose points of view went on to define the way the Indian Constitution would identify Scheduled Castes.

In Galanter's analytic framework, caste has been legally understood and organised through three principal models or frames. As he has termed them, these are the sacral, sectarian and associational frames of conceptually structuring and deploying caste. To elaborate, sacral accounts posit caste groups as constituent parts of a unified Hindu religious order. In this frame, Hindu society is seen as a differentiated but integrated order of caste groups all of whom are held together by the unifying force of axiomatically applied scriptural doctrines. The sectarian frame posits caste as an independent religious community demarcated by its own doctrines, rituals or culture. This model conceives of caste as a religious unit but one that is self-contained and disassociated from a larger religious order. The rights and duties of the group and its members follow from its own rules and practices and not from its place in a larger axiomatically and scripturally organised Hindu sacral order. Lastly, in the associational frame, caste is understood as a self-governing group, which is marked neither by a fixed place in a larger religious order nor by distinctive religious beliefs or practices. The bonds of association in this last frame might include religion, but this is to be understood merely as one among many other aspects of group life.[24]

Each of these models as they detail an understanding of caste has played important functional roles in the British colonial state. Thus, in the organisation of religious personal laws, castes were viewed through the lens of the sacral frame. In this frame castes were seen to be part of an integrated order of Hindu communities divided along the lines of twice-born, or *dvija*, communities to whom one set of personal laws applied, and lower-born *sudra* communities to whom a different set of personal laws applied.

This distinction of caste groups into *dvija*s and *sudra*s turns on the assumption that various *jati*s, *sampradaya*s, *jamat*s, and so on, that define social life in India can be pulled together by authoritative doctrines of the classical texts of Hindu law. These texts and their doctrines are said to axiomatically organise Hindu society through the classical category of *varna*, which pulled together the multitude of castes groups into four hierarchically organised groups or *varna*s – *brahmin*s, *kshatriya*s, *vaisya*s and *sudra*s. The *brahmin*, *kshatriya and vaisya varna*s comprised the *dvija*s, while the *sudra*s were ritually inferior to the other three groups.

Slotting the multitude of Indian castes into appropriate *varna*s is no easy task and has required courts to device ways in which they could distinguish between the *brahmin, kshatriya* or *vaisya varna*s from the *sudra varna*. In some cases, the test to identify a group was the customary practices said to be typical of the *sudra*s. In others, the identification of *varna* took place by evaluation of the caste group's own consciousness of its status and the acceptance of this estimate by other castes in the locality. Often, these estimations of status were tied to notions of purity and pollution practices between caste groups.[25] However, in all these cases castes are seen as religious entities that 'occupy their respective places in the sacral order of ranks which embraces all groups within a doctrinally and axiomatically understood Hinduism'.[26]

On the other hand, as self-governing entities with powers of internal self-government recognised by the colonial government, castes were organised as sectarian and associational entities[27] (models of caste that this chapter will treat as variants of each other). These self-governing powers of caste were primarily enforced by colonial courts to protect caste privileges and to defend group control through practices like excommunication. Even so, it is important to note that sectarian and the associational models of caste were equally plausible ways of understanding and representing caste in colonial government as was the sacral model. In the sectarian and associational models, caste was the basis of social organisation and could include all manner of groups with established patterns of social organisation. And, as Galanter has shown, this could also include non-Hindu groups, with courts having recognised castes among Muslims, Parsis, Jains, Sikhs and Christians.[28]

As caste gradually began to get drawn into representative politics of colonial India, both sacral and the sectarian and associational models of caste were equally available to identify caste groups as candidates for representation in government. To some extent this was apparent in the clash of the opposing positions in the Poona Pact that was seemingly resolved in favour of the sacral model. However, as independence approached, Galanter argues, the problem resurfaced but that the sacral approach to caste was overshadowed by the influence of the other two approaches. Galanter attributes this to two reasons. First, the passage of the Hindu Code Bill, which established a uniform Hindu law for all Hindus and rendered *varna* insignificant as a legal category. Second, the constitutional abolition of untouchability in Article 17 was also intended to make *varna* to irrelevant in the legal and administrative practice of independent India.

However, the eclipse of *varna* in ordering personal law or even the abolition of untouchability has not pushed aside the sacralised framework of caste. On the contrary, as the discussions in the Constituent Assembly illustrate, a sacralised Hindu identification of castes continued to play a determining role in conceiving the challenge that caste posed for the new Constitution. Most significantly, this model of caste was carried into the working of Article 341 of the Constitution, which authorised the president or parliament to identify the castes that would secure constitutional recognition.

The exercise of presidential power under Article 341 has taken the shape of the Constitution (Scheduled Castes) Order, 1950, which specifies that 'no person professing a religion different from Hinduism shall be deemed to be a member of the Scheduled Castes'.[29] This demarcation of caste is key to identifying caste groups eligible to avail themselves of the benefits of the Constitution's programme for the social transformation of caste disability. Prima facie this account of caste and caste injustice betrays a sacral account of caste. However, the sacral imprint of modelling caste in this fashion is usefully elaborated through judicial decisions that are outlined in the following section.

Scheduled Caste Identity and Caste Disability in the Courts

The Scheduled Castes Order issued under Article 341 identifies over a thousand erstwhile untouchable caste groups as eligible for the various ameliorative programmes administered by the Indian state as well as for quotas reserved in legislatures. Administering these rights demands a method for identifying and delineating the caste groups that can be said to be untouchables, and this has never been an easy task.[30] Bracketing the complex procedural process of identifying erstwhile untouchable castes, this chapter will only emphasise the threshold eligibility requirement that they be identified as part of the Hindu religion. Doing so, this section illustrates the sacral account of caste that is implicit in this form of identifying caste communities. More importantly, this section also demonstrates the manner in which this sacral account of caste reinforces a communal representation of the Indian people that this book seeks to foreground.

The principal challenge posed by the identification of caste as a problem of Hindu society is its inability to recognise the assertion by individuals who self-identify as members of caste groups but do so in sectarian or associational frames. At any rate, these groups do not understand caste only as a sacral phenomenon held together by the axiomatic authority of Hindu Law. On the contrary, these groups view caste as a socio-structural phenomenon that cannot be reduced to parochial problems of any one religious group. The problem these groups highlight is perhaps most apparent in the case of religious converts who suffer de facto from all the disabilities flowing from untouchability, but classified as faiths other than 'Hinduism', they are deemed ineligible for the rights reserved by the Constitution for the Scheduled Castes.

As an early decision of the Supreme Court that addresses the effects of conversion from the Hindu community, *S. Rajagopal v. C. M. Armugam*[31] foregrounds judicial justification of the exclusion of non-Hindu communities from the list of Scheduled Castes.[32] In this case, the parliamentary election of the appellant S. Rajgopal, a candidate claiming to belong to the Adi Dravida Scheduled Caste community, from a reserved constituency in the erstwhile State of Mysore, was challenged on the grounds that he had converted to Christianity. It was alleged that his conversion made him ineligible to avail himself of the Scheduled Caste quota to fight elections. Rajgopal claimed that he never converted to Christianity, and even if it were proved that he had converted, he contended that he had reconverted before the relevant election date.

The court held that he converted to Christianity and that there was no evidence that he had reconverted to being a Hindu and was therefore ineligible to contest the election from the Scheduled Caste constituency. The court's reasoning was of course framed by the Scheduled Castes Order which was justified almost entirely in sacral and doctrinal terms. Thus, finding that he had converted to Christianity, the court stated that

> when the appellant embraced Christianity in 1949, he lost the membership of the Adi Dravida Hindu caste. *The Christian religion does not recognise any caste classifications.* All Christians are treated as equals and there is no distinction between one Christian and another of the type that is recognised between members of different castes belonging to Hindu religion. *In fact, caste system prevails only amongst Hindus or possibly in some religions closely allied to the Hindu religion like Sikhism....* It must, therefore, be held that, when the appellant got

converted to Christianity in 1949, he ceased to belong to the Adi Dravida caste.[33] (Emphasis added)

In other words, conversion is framed as a sacral act that detaches individuals from preceding social relations. Consequently, as a matter of scripture and doctrine, caste was understood to be present in Hindu traditions but absent in Christianity. However, drawing on Galanter, caste could also be understood to be akin to a sectarian and associational community defined by relevant patterns of co-mingling and interaction. From this perspective various communities have argued that doctrinal tenets have no necessary or axiomatic bearing on the way they are framed by the disabilities arising from caste society and its practice of untouchability.

In some cases courts have obliquely acknowledged the possibility that caste survives conversion. However, the structure of the Scheduled Castes Order and the general assumptions guiding the identification of castes leave courts with very few options. Consider, for instance, the Supreme Court's decision in *Soosai v. Union of India*[34] where the court heard a constitutional challenge to the Scheduled Castes Order of 1950.

Soosai, the petitioner in this case, was a cobbler who belonged to the Adi Dravida Scheduled Caste community but had converted to Christianity. Consequently, under the Scheduled Castes Order he was judged ineligible to receive certain welfare schemes of the Government of India. Soosai challenged the Scheduled Castes Order on the ground that it violated constitutional guarantees of equality and freedom to practise religion. Soosai argued that he remained an Adi Dravida as a matter of sociological fact and that differential treatment only because of his conversion would result in the violation of the Constitution's equality provisions as well as his right to religious freedom. In advancing these normative claims Soosai also contended that caste survives conversion and that caste disability is independent of a sacralised and axiomatic view of the Hindu religion.

Responding to Soosai's contention that the exclusion of Christians in the Scheduled Castes Order was discriminatory, the Supreme Court demanded that

it must be shown that they suffer from a comparable depth of social and economic disabilities and cultural and educational backwardness and similar levels of degradation within the Christian community necessitating intervention by the State under the provisions of the Constitution. It is not sufficient to show that the same caste continues after conversion. It is necessary to establish further that the disabilities and handicaps suffered from such caste membership in the social order of its origin – Hinduism – continue in their oppressive severity in the new environment of a different religion's community.[35]

Having held that no such evidence was submitted, the court was able to dismiss Soosai's claims. Even so, the court does entertain the possibility that caste disability survives conversion thereby showing itself to be willing to consider Soosai's claims if he could demonstrate that he continued to suffer the same set of disabilities within the Christian community as he did before his conversion. It might well have been possible to establish that he suffered caste disabilities within the Christian community. In fact, this might be one of the ways in which a Christian Scheduled Caste could suffer from caste disability.[36] Nevertheless, this is not quite how Soosai presented his case in court. That is, it was his case that he was entitled to be recognised as a Scheduled Caste on the ground that he continued to be discriminated against as an Adi Dravida and therefore the exclusion of Adi Dravidas who converted to Christianity constituted a violation of the Constitution's promise of equal treatment.

A case like *Soosai* points to the ambiguity regarding the relevant community in relation to which the determination of caste disability must be determined. Was it his identity as an Adi Dravida or was it his identity as an Adi Dravida Christian? To the extent that the court was open to evidence of discrimination it suggested that it was not conclusively wedded to a doctrinal and axiomatic Hindu account of caste. However, to the extent that it required Soosai to show that he faced discrimination even upon conversion the court fell back on a sacral conception of caste that presumed that Christianity doctrinally effaced caste, a presumption that could be rebutted with evidence. Consequently, to this extent the court continued to be in the thrall of a sacral model.

Soosai was a rare case where the court made a detailed examination of the constitutionality of the Scheduled Castes Order and the grounds on which that Order could be defended. However, most cases relating to the identification of Scheduled Castes reaffirmed the sacral model that organised the Order. Therefore, to sum up the manner in which the sacral model has overdetermined the identification of caste, it is useful to consider cases of reconversion back into the Hindu community by erstwhile untouchables. In these cases, courts have devised what they have called the doctrine of eclipse through which they have held that conversion only eclipses caste disabilities which reinstate on return or reconversion to the Hindu community.[37] To draw on one such decision in the *K. P. Manu case*:

[W]hen a person is converted to Christianity or some other religion the original caste remains under eclipse and as soon as during his/her lifetime the person is reconverted to the original religion the eclipse disappears and the caste automatically revives.[38]

The absurdity of this position is only too obvious. That is, it is only when a person's identity within a sacralised conception of the Hindu community is established that concomitant facts arising out of caste injustice become relevant. In addition, cases like *K. P. Manu* demonstrate the manner in which caste inequity ensuing from sectarian and associational social forms are pushed aside to firmly establish a sacral Hindu model of caste in Indian constitutional practice.

This approach to caste has not gone politically unchallenged. That is, the unfairness of excluding social groups subject to similar disabilities as the constitutionally recognised Scheduled Castes has been resisted by excluded groups. This has resulted in the progressive expansion of the Scheduled Castes Order over the years to include communities beyond the 'Hindu' fold. Thus, all Sikh untouchables were included in 1956 and Buddhist untouchables were included in 1990. In relation to these later developments it could be said that they were possible as they pertain to what are understood to be largely 'home grown' religious traditions. Muslims and Christians have not enjoyed the same latitude, and continue to be excluded from recognition as Scheduled Castes.

However, the Ranganath Mishra Commission on minority rights has recommended that Article 341 be expanded to include untouchables from among Muslims and Christians as well.[39] Therefore, it is conceivable that the Scheduled Castes Order could at some future point also include caste groups from all religious persuasions and not just those identified within the fold of the Hindu community. However, even as such an extension of the Scheduled Castes Order could result in the de-sacralisation of caste identification, it is also important to note the difficulty in pushing aside the sacral accounts of caste. This is so because of the conceptual depth of sacralised religious identities as they have determined constitutional debates detailed in previous chapters, as well as the way it has been extended to the identification of the 'Backward Classes', another significant constitutionally recognised group subject to the ameliorative or the transformative programme of the Indian constitutional state. It is this extension of the sacralised model of caste to the identification of the 'Backward Classes' that must now be discussed to illustrate the entrenchment of the sacral and Hindu conceptualisation of caste in Indian constitutional practice.

Sacralisation of Caste in the identification of 'Backward Classes'

The term 'Backward Classes', as briefly noted earlier in this chapter, was a technical term in colonial government and in many princely states. Groups so identified were eligible for special benefits in government. In addition, as scholars note, in some instances the term included the Depressed Classes to constitute a broad spectrum of backward castes.[40] In other instances, the term referred to castes understood to be a rung higher than the Depressed Classes but who were for social and economic reasons understood to be backward.[41] However, at least from the Government of India Act of 1935 a clear distinction emerged between the Backward Classes and the Depressed Classes.

By the time the new Constitution was being discussed, the objectives resolution as proposed by Nehru made clear this distinction when it proposed special measures for 'minorities, backward and tribal areas, and *depressed and other backward classes*'[42] (emphasis added). As a term that had limited currency in much of northern India, delegates from these areas to the Constituent Assembly expressed their surprise at the inclusion of a phrase so vague. By contrast, as a term of art in the government practices of large parts of southern and western India, the delegates from Madras, Mysore and Bombay reassured their northern colleagues that backwardness was indeed a technical term through which a range of caste groups found representation in government.[43]

Consequently, backwardness as a distinct axis to ameliorate the concerns of groups so recognised was drawn into the Constitution in Article 16(4) and later, by way of amendment, in Articles 15(4) and 15(5). Article 15(4) permits the state to undertake special measures for the advancement of 'socially and educationally backward classes' of citizens, Article 15(5) permits state action for the advancement of the interests of 'socially and educationally backward classes' of citizens in educational institutions, while Article 16(4) makes provision for the representation of 'backward classes' of citizens in public employment. As apparent, the qualifying terms describing the Backward Classes are slightly different across Articles 15 and 16. However, this discussion will treat them as broadly interchangeable.[44] Further, as these provisions suggest, the thrust of this constitutional ambition to advance the interests of citizens belonging to the 'backward classes' have revolved around their greater inclusion in state-funded educational institutions and in government employment. Commenting on this broad area of constitutional practice, this section examines aspects of the institutional challenge of demarcating and identifying the backwardness in Articles 15 and 16.

Backwardness had no defined place in the constitutional text at the time of its adoption even though there was a broad consensus that the constitutional project empowered the state to advance the interests of the Backward Classes. Further, though the Constitution explicitly facilitated the representation of 'Backward Classes' in public employment at the time of its adoption, there was no similar provision to permit state action for the Backward Classes in matters of education.[45] However, as various provincial governments sought to facilitate the entry of Backward Classes in state-supported educational institutions the absence of a specific constitutional provision empowering such action emerged as a problem.

This problem was an important part of the *Champakam Dorairajan*[46] case, where the Supreme Court had to decide whether a government scheme providing quotas in higher education for all major caste groups in the state of Madras state violated the constitutional commitment to equality. Noting the absence of a specific provision like Article 16(4) empowering special provisions for Backward Classes, as also the bar imposed by provisions like Article 29(2),[47] the scheme was struck down as constitutionally impermissible. However, the decision upset the quotas previously available for Backward Classes in southern India under the colonial state, sparking a movement that culminated in the addition of Article 15(4) through the first amendment to the Indian Constitution. In turn, this constitutional provision cleared ground to permit the government to undertake special provisions for the Backward Classes both in education and in public employment. However, their identification remained a problem and is the key concern of this section.

The precise contours of the identification of Backward Classes are an extremely complex field. Of that broader field this section only foregrounds the extent to which Backward Classes are identified as caste groups.[48] Backward Classes are not necessarily synonymous with backward castes. However, by and large, historical practice has identified Backward Classes in Articles 15 and 16 with backward castes. There have of course also been efforts to consider other axes of demarcating backwardness which have attempted to frame approaches to backwardness beyond the frame of caste. In constitutional practice these have included other identity-based criteria such as religion as well as non-identity based criteria such as income, education levels and geographic location. But, despite these efforts, caste has continued to remain the most significant social unit directing government policy aimed at advancing the interests of those identified as socially Backward Classes.

However, even as caste has framed the identification of backwardness, the absence of a clear constitutional definition of backwardness meant that its demarcation had to be devised through evolving administrative and adjudicative practice. Thus, examining the constitutional validity of ameliorative government schemes for groups designated as backward, Indian courts have played an important role in demarcating the criteria for the identification of Backward Classes. Consequently, examining judicial accounts of caste as an axis of determining social backwardness in a few landmark decisions, it is possible to illustrate the form in which the judiciary has both characterised backwardness and specified the place of caste within its account of a Backward Class.

The specification of caste as an axis to specify backwardness does not of itself clear the fog around the identification of backwardness. Thus, there are a range of debates, for instance, on the different criteria of identification across the central and the state governments, the extent to which caste ought to determine backwardness, as also the data that authenticates the extent to which special provisions can be made on behalf of the Backward Classes.[49] Of these issues, this section only narrows down on a tendency in judicial interpretation that echoes the sacral and Hindu nature of caste. Nonetheless, as a view arising in important cases, it is a tendency of note, besides of course echoing the broader argument that this chapter makes about the sacralisation of caste.

Thus, in the landmark decision *M. R. Balaji v. State of Mysore*,[50] the Supreme Court was called on to decide the constitutionality of a government scheme provisioning quotas for socially and educationally Backward Classes in government-affiliated institutions of higher education. Interpreting the power of the government to make such quota, the court was clear that Article 15(4) granted the state to make special provisions as long as it was consistent with the Constitution's equality commitments. In particular, it held that provisions made for the Backward Classes under Article 15(4) were to be understood to be an exception to 15(1) and could not amount to being a fraud on the Constitution's broader commitment to equality.

Bracketing the normative detail of the court's opinion on this quota scheme it is useful to emphasise the manner in which it addressed the identification of socially and economically Backward Classes. Addressing social backwardness, the court traced the problem of backwardness to Hindu social structure and the place of caste within Hindu society. In the normative scheme of the court's decision, it was held that caste could not be the sole determinant of backwardness as this would entrench caste in constitutionally impermissible ways.

However, it also made a sociological assertion about caste that is particularly important. That is, it asserted that caste could not be the sole determinant of backwardness because

> if the caste of the group of citizens was made the sole basis for determining the social backwardness of the said group, that test would inevitably break down in relation to many sections of Indian society which do not recognise castes in the conventional sense known to Hindu society. How is one going to decide whether Muslims, Christians or Jains, or even Lingayats are socially backward or not? The test of castes would be inapplicable to those groups, but that would hardly justify the exclusion of these groups in toto from the operation of Art. 15(4).[51] (Emphasis added)

That is, caste was understood as a sacral bond that excluded non-Hindu communities such as Muslims, Christians and even Jains and Lingayats. Thus, insofar as the court was willing to recognise backwardness in these non-Hindu communities it would have to be identified through criteria other than caste. Presumably, these could include income, educational levels, hereditary occupation, and so on. However, even in the case of caste, as the court held that it was normatively impermissible to organise a scheme for special provisions solely on the basis of caste, backwardness in Hindu groups also would have to be supplemented by other evidence of backwardness such as educational backwardness, and so on. Thus, states seeking to affirmatively act on behalf of Backward Classes were obliged to generate data about caste groups to demonstrate backwardness on social, economic, and educational grounds. Even so, the court's conception of social backwardness was framed by a sacralised or doctrinal Hindu conception of caste.[52]

Since the *Balaji* case in the early 1960s, ameliorative programmes for the Backward Classes have been backed by considerable study of the conditions of various groups assumed to be backward. Extensive reports of Backward Classes commissions at both the central and state levels have produced a wealth of information on the identification and administration of programmes for the Backward Classes. In various instances, Muslim and Christian groups have also been included as part of backward caste groups deserving of special measures under Articles 15 and 16 of the Constitution.[53] However, it is important to clarify that the extension of backwardness to Muslim and Christian groups did not imply that caste was the grounds on which their backwardness was established and recognised. That is, where caste has been an axis for the determination of backwardness, courts and public institutions have for the most part operated with the assumption that caste is a sacralised Hindu phenomenon.

In this context it is useful to consider the debate generated by the Mandal Commission or the second report of the Backward Classes Commission appointed by the Union government whose recommendations included provision for a 27 per cent employment quota in the central government and its undertakings for the Backward Classes. This report was accepted by the central government in 1990, triggering an important judicial battle that was resolved by the Supreme Court in the *Indra Sawhney* judgment.[54]

As a landmark decision resolving a range of issues pertaining to the constitutionality of reservations for the Backward Classes, the *Indra Sawhney* decision also addressed the challenge of identifying backward social groups. Of the plurality of decisions that constituted this judgment, the decision by Justice Jeevan Reddy is an important one expressing the majority opinion of the court. Therefore, drawing on his decision it is again instructive to examine the way he ties caste into the identification of backwardness.

According to Justice Reddy, the challenge that caste posed to the egalitarian ethos of the Indian Constitution was its constitutive role in the Hindu religion which was

> not known for its egalitarian ethos. It divided its adherents into four watertight compartments. Those outside this four tier system (chaturvarna) were the outcastes (Panchamas), the lowliest.... The fourth, shudras, were no better, though certainly better than the Panchamas. The lowliness attached to them (Shudras and Panchamas) by virtue of their birth in these castes, unconnected with their deeds..... Poverty there has been ... in every country. But none had the misfortune of having this social division – or as some call it, degradation – super-imposed on poverty.[55]

As obvious from the extract, castes are treated as social groups within a sacralised and *varna*-based conception of the Hindu religion. Justice Reddy paints this *varna*-based organisation of Indian society as the 'stark reality notwithstanding all our protestations and abhorrence and all attempts at weeding out this phenomenon'.[56] Restating Justice Reddy's assertions in Galanter's conceptual framework as it has guided this chapter, the sacral order of Hindu society is the background assumption directing the identification of castes that could be considered backward for the purposes of Articles 15(4), 15(5) and 16(4).

However, as cases from the *Balaji* decision have held, a caste by itself would not qualify for constitutional recognition as a Backward Class unless it was also established that it was a socially and educationally backward group. Various decisions after *Balaji* have differently emphasised the extent to which caste was to be a criterion to determine backwardness. Some cases like *Balaji* itself have held caste to be a relevant criterion, others have held that caste can be the sole criterion to identify backwardness, and Indra Sawhney itself has held that caste can be a dominant criteria to determine backwardness.[57] Further, Justice Reddy himself has noted that that Christian and Muslim groups could be also be recognised to be backward classes where the evidence points in that direction.[58] However, none of this takes away from the background assumption of caste as a sacralised and axiomatically organised Hindu phenomenon, and castes as backward classes being social groups located along the hierarchical contours of a Hindu religious order.

Important scholarship has noted that this association of backward classes to a sacralised account of caste is perhaps more appropriately applied to Scheduled Castes who have been historically discriminated and have suffered the ignominy of untouchability.[59] This is especially so as Backward Classes have not suffered such discrimination, and in many cases backward classes are the locally dominant castes. However, from the point of view of this chapter, the sacralisation of caste presents this foundational problem of the Indian constitutional republic being addressed and resolved in parochial Hindu terms. As noticed earlier it is possible that the intersection of backwardness and caste could be characterised in more neutral terms through sectarian or associational accounts of caste. However, framed by the sacral account and the broader communal background outlined in this book, backwardness as it bears on caste has also been largely resolved in communal and Hindu terms. Therefore, it is on this note that the strands of this chapter must be pulled together to a conclusion.

Conclusion

Carrying forward the argument of this book, this chapter has demonstrated that the constitutional challenge of caste injustice was resolved primarily as the redemption of Hindu society for the evils it inflicted on lower castes. Caste was and is a constituent problem for the Indian republic, and efforts that the Constitution expends on the problem of caste is no clearer than in Article 17 that seeks to abolish the practice of untouchability. However, untouchability and the other inequities of caste society are problems that suffuse the fabric of

Indian society and are not problems facing any one parochial group. Even so, constitutional practice has conceived of caste and those suffering the inequities of caste as a sacralised Hindu problem. It is this sacralisation of caste as it mirrors and ties into communal identities generated in other constitutional debates that this book has detailed in this and previous chapters.

The sacralised Hindu account of caste is only one way of understanding the problem of caste society and the inequities it underwrites. As this chapter has noted, there are other equally plausible forms of modelling caste as sectarian or associational communities. The extent to which the characterisation of caste as sectarian and associational communities can redress or better address the structural violence of caste is of course barely addressed in this chapter. On the other hand, this chapter has merely pointed to the manner in which a sacralised representation of caste has borne the burden of characterising the problem of caste in Indian constitutional practice. In turn this sacralised account of caste ties into and echoes the communal representation of the Indian people detailed in both this and previous chapters.

Notes

1. Chapter 3.
2. Eleanor Mae Zelliot, 'Dr. Ambedkar and the Mahar Movement' (Philadelphia: University of Pennsylvania, 1969), 139, https://repository. upenn.edu/dissertations/AAI6921466, accessed 8 November 2022.
3. Cited in Mark Galanter, *Competing Equality: Law and the Backward Classes in India* (Berkeley: University of California Press, 1984), 21.
4. Galanter traces the nationalisation of the caste question to the grouping of lower castes under the rubric of untouchability and identifies the first pan-national use of the term 'untouchable' to the Maharajah of Baroda's address to the Bombay Depressed Classes Mission in 1909. Galanter, *Competing Equality*, 24.
5. Galanter, *Competing Equality*, 26–27.
6. A position endorsed by many others. For example, see Dirks, *Castes of Mind*.
7. Nicholas B Dirks, 'Castes of Mind', *Representations* 37 (Winter 1992): 56.
8. Dirks, 'Castes of Mind', 67.
9. Dirks, 'Castes of Mind'.
10. Herbert Risley, *The People of India*, ed. William Crooke (2nd edn, New Delhi: Asian Educational Services, 1999), 278.
11. Morley mentions that Ameer Ali, as part of a delegation of Muslims who met him in regard to the 1909 reforms, petitioned him to exclude large

numbers of the lower castes from being counted as Hindus. John Morley, *Indian Speeches (1907–1909)* (London: Macmillan, 1909), 102. Galanter similarly points out Muslim support for the 1911 census commissioner who suggested that the untouchables or the Depressed Classes be enumerated separately from the Hindus. Galanter, *Competing Equality*, 25.

12.   Galanter, *Competing Equality*, 26. See also Zelliot, 'Dr. Ambedkar and the Mahar Movement'; V. Geetha and S. V. Rajadurai, *Towards a Non-Brahmin Millennium: From Iyothee Thass to Periyar* (Calcutta: Samya, 1998).

13.   Galanter, *Competing Equality*, 18–41, 121–53.

14.   For example, see Char, *Readings in the Constitutional History of India*; Coupland, *Report on the Constitutional Problem in India*.

15.   Char, *Readings in the Constitutional History of India*, 557–60.

16.   Char, *Readings in the Constitutional History of India*, 552–54.

17.   Under the Poona Pact the number of seats reserved for the Depressed Classes would be considerably more than what was provided in the Communal Award. The principle of separate electorates would be applicable but only at a preliminary stage of the elections where the voters of the Depressed Classes would elect a panel of candidates from which members of the legislature would be elected by the general body of Hindu voters, including those of the Depressed Classes. Char, *Readings in the Constitutional History of India*, 560–63. See also Coupland, *Report on the Constitutional Problem in India*, 128.

18.   Among the measures undertaken by the state under Artice 15(4), quotas in institutions of higher learning have produced disputes involving the highest stakes in contemporary India.

19.   *Constituent Assembly Debates: Official Report*, vol. 5 (New Delhi: Lok Sabha Secretariat, 1999), 227–28.

20.   *Constituent Assembly Debates: Official Report*, vol. 10 (New Delhi: Lok Sabha Secretariat, 1999), 247.

21.   *Constituent Assembly Debates: Official Report*, vol. 10, 232–36.

22.   See, for example, the comments of P. R. Thakur in the Constituent Assembly, *Constituent Assembly of India Debates (Proceedings)*, vol. 3, 1 May 1947, https://www.constitutionofindia.net/constitution_assembly_debates/volume/3/1947-05-01, accessed 27 October 2022.

23.   For example, the comments of Muniswami Pillai, *Constituent Assembly Debates: Official Report*, vol. 9 (New Delhi: Lok Sabha Secretariat, 1999), 1638–39.

24.   Marc Galanter, 'Religious Aspects of Caste', in *South Asian Politics and Religion*, Donald Eugene Smith, 278–79 (Princeton: Princeton University Press, 1966).

25. Galanter, 'Religious Aspects of Caste', 280–82.

26. Galanter, 'Religious Aspects of Caste', 282.

27. See, for example, Amrita Shodhan, *A Question of Community: Religious Groups and Colonial Law* (Calcutta: Samya, 2001).

28. See, for instance, cases like *Abdul Kadir v. Dharma* 20 Bom. 190 (1895), cited in Galanter, 'Religious Aspects of Caste', 289.

29. Galanter, *Competing Equality*, 304. The Constitution (Scheduled Castes) Order, 1950, was amended in 1956 and 1990 and now reads that 'no person who professes a religion different from the Hindu, the Sikh or the Buddhist religion shall be deemed to be a member of a Scheduled Caste'.

30. Simon Charsley, '"Untouchable": What Is in a Name?' *Journal of the Royal Anthropological Institute* 2, no. 1 (1996): 1.

31. *S. Rajagopal v. C. M. Armugam* AIR 1969 SC 101.

32. The cases discussed on this point are only illustrative and this is not an exhaustive survey of the judicial landscape in this field, especially the many High Court decisions on this point. Therefore, it is only to be expected that the Supreme Court cases discussed were preceded by important lower court decisions. For example, in *Michael v. Venkataswaran* AIR 1952 Mad 474 and *In re Thomas* AIR 1953 Mad. 21 the court held that rights granted to the Scheduled Castes could not be claimed by Christians because the Christian religion does not recognise caste. In both cases the courts were also reluctant to review the constitutionality of the Presidential Order notifying Scheduled Castes by stating that it was beyond the reach of the courts.

33. *S. Rajagopal v. C. M. Armugam*, 107.

34. *Soosai v. Union of India* MANU/SC/0045/1985.

35. *Soosai v. Union of India*.

36. For instances of a case of discrimination within the Christian community on grounds of caste, see *Kattalai Michael Pillai and Ors. vs Right Reverend J.M. Barthe, S.J. Bishop of Trichinopoly and Ors.* AIR 1917 Mad 431.

37. For example, see *S. Anbalagan v B. Devarajan & Ors* (1984) 2 SCC 112; *Kailash Sonkar v. Maya Devi* (1984) 2 SCC 91; *Principal Guntur v. Mohan Rao* (1976) 3 SCC 411. For effects of the adoption of a different Hindu denomination, see *Chitturbhuj Vithaldas Jasani v Moreshwar Parashram & Ors* 1954 AIR 236.

38. MANU/SC/0189/2015.

39. Ranganath Misra, 'Report of the National Commission for Religious and Linguistic Minorities'(New Delhi: Ministry of Minority Affairs 2007), https://www.sabrangindia.in/reports/2007-delhi-report-national-commission-religious-and-linguistic-minorities-ranganath-misra, accessed 8 November 2022.

40. Galanter, *Competing Equality*; Zelliot, 'Dr. Ambedkar and the Mahar Movement'; Geetha and Rajadurai, *Towards a Non-Brahmin Millennium*.

41. Galanter, *Competing Equality*, 153–59.

42. Galanter, *Competing Equality*, 158.

43. Galanter, *Competing Equality*, 154–58.

44. Vinay Sitapati, 'Reservations', in *The Oxford Handbook of the Indian Constitution*, ed. Sujit Choudhry, Madhav Khosla and Pratap Bhanu Mehta, 720–41 (New Delhi: Oxford University Press, 2016).

45. Both Articles 15(4) and 15(5) were incorporated into the constitution by way of amendment.

46. *State of Madras v. Champakam Dorairajan* AIR 1951 SC 226.

47. Article 29(2) states, 'No citizen shall be denied admission into any educational institution maintained by the State or receiving aid out of State funds on grounds only of religion, race, caste, language or any of them.'

48. See Galanter, *Competing Equality*; Laura Dudley Jenkins, *Identity and Identification in India* (London: Routledge, 2003).

49. Sitapati, 'Reservations', 722–24.

50. *M. R. Balaji v. State of Mysore* AIR 1963 SC 649.

51. *M. R. Balaji v. State of Mysore*.

52. Galanter, *Competing Equality*, 188–204.

53. Galanter, *Competing Equality*; Sitapati (n 234).

54. *Indra Sawhney v. Union of India* MANU/SC/0104/1993.

55. *Indra Sawhney v. Union of India*, para 2.

56. *Indra Sawhney v. Union of India*, para 82.

57. Sitapati, *Reservations*, 723.

58. *Indra Sawhney v. Union of India*, para 83.

59. André Béteille, *The Backward Classes in Contemporary India* (Delhi: Oxford University Press 1992), 85–86.

Conclusion

Appraising the Communal Constitution

To sum up and draw this book to a conclusion, the Communal Constitution was introduced as a pathological tendency in Indian constitutional practice that identified the Indian people along religious lines. Normatively, this presents a straightforward problem pointing to the task of defending, justifying, and pulling constitutional practice back to the Indian Constitution's much-celebrated promise of equal liberties. However, to make explicit the contours of the Communal Constitution, this book has consistently bracketed off and distanced its gaze from the search for normatively preferred or correct solutions. In the place of normative argument the previous chapters have emphasised communal aspects in constitutional design and practice that have belied and cohabited with the Constitution's much-celebrated liberal ambitions. Even so, as the Communal Constitution acquires salience against the background of the Constitution's liberal values, those aspirations also set the ground along which the discussion of the previous chapters is best appraised.

The Liberal Background

With the hindsight of the previous chapters, the Communal Constitution could be described as a frustration or even critique of liberal secular aspirations as it has operated in Indian constitutional practice. The hegemonic grasp of liberal secular ideas is under severe stress both in India and in all parts of the modern world. In everyday politics a surge in populist authoritarian and nationalist movements attempts to dismantle the open and fraternal institutional culture that makes equal liberties possible.[1] In the realm of ideas, liberal secular values have always been subject to challenge.[2] However, this has been especially so over the last few decades with a significant body of scholarship pointing to various challenges or impossibilities in engendering and fostering liberal secular politics. This body of work is too large and varied to meaningfully recount, but it is important to mention that its emphasis on a critical reconstruction of liberal secular norms as they have been shaped and passed on by state practice forms an important backdrop to this book's account of the Communal Constitution.[3] Accordingly, exploring the imprint of religion on how the Indian people are identified, all previous chapters have attempted to make salient the challenges posed to the Indian Constitution's bid to demarcate its people as a liberal community of free and equal citizens.

Thus, as the previous chapters have shown, the equal liberty of citizens has not always been the preferred choice to delimit the identity of the Indian people. This problem has been illustrated through discussions on religious liberty, personal law, minority rights and the identification of castes as they are tied to the remnant of a colonial constitutional imagination that cohabits with the liberal Constitution and which casts the Indian people as a collection of religious communities. In turn, the continued grasp of this colonial frame over contemporary constitutional practice has been the principal problem that previous chapters have detailed.

Evaluating the Communal Constitution

Drawing on previous discussions, there are three themes that this concluding section will emphasise as it evaluates the significance of the Communal Constitution for Indian Constitution studies. First, the conceptual frame, and hopefully the conceptual clarity, that the Communal Constitution brings to studying alternative forms of representing the Indian people in constitutional design and practice. Second, the limits of 'the people' as a frame to authorise sovereign political authority over the staggering social diversity that obtains in South Asian societies like India. Third, the value of the Communal Constitution to the normative study and practice of the Indian Constitution. Each of these themes is now discussed in turn as a way of pulling together the themes discussed in this book as also to speculate in small measure on those that have been glossed over.

Rethinking Community

Most importantly for Indian Constitution studies, the Communal Constitution makes visible alternative bids to constitute political community and the forms in which they have drawn on the sovereign authority of the Indian people. As the overwhelmingly dominant normative background that shapes the contemporary Constitution, the liberal bid to fashion the Indian people as a community of individual citizens could be easily misunderstood to be the only form of political community that the Constitution recognises.

With notable exceptions,[4] much scholarship echoes this presumption either by pressing for a broadly liberal vision of the people premised on equal liberty[5] or by characterising the Constitution as a break from the past that entrenched a liberal vision of the people.[6] This book has resisted this presumption to argue and demonstrate its case for the continued significance of the Communal Constitution. But more importantly, in doing so it also brings to light a contested field of candidates that have pitched themselves as alternative candidates to identify the Indian people.

The most obvious alternative candidate that has been extensively discussed across all chapters has been the representation of India as a fragmented political community made up of religious groups divided by their essential and axiomatic scriptural truths. As previous chapters have shown, this is a classic colonial representation of the Indian people. Drawing on this colonial account of India, nationalist assertion has spawned important analogues that have identified the national mainstream as Hindu but set against a range of minorities of whom Muslims have historically been the most significant.

Further, differing conceptual weights accorded to Hindus, Muslims and others have, for the most part, produced the spectrum of options along which the Indian people have been articulated in Indian constitutional politics. In his field-defining work, Partha Chatterjee comprehensively maps and identifies these options in modern Indian history as the communal-nationalist, liberal secular, plural, and regional accounts of organising the Indian people.[7] When the polity was cast as embodying Hindu and Muslim identities, the people were articulated in communal and nationalist terms; when identities such as Hindu and Muslim were subordinated to that of equal citizenship, the people were identified as liberal and secular; when Hindu, Muslim or other identities were cast as part of a civilisational legacy of social diversity, people were identified with a plural polity; and when the polity was identified with local and provincial identities, the people were identified in regional and later federal idioms.

Each of these forms of identifying the people can also be associated with important historical moments. Thus, the communal-nationalist form of identifying the people is the earliest modern form in which the Indian people were represented both by the colonial state and in nationalist assertion. Further, as the chapters of this book have sought to argue, communal-nationalist accounts of the Indian people continue to slip into and frame contemporary constitutional debates on religious freedom, personal laws, minority rights and caste identity.

Even as the book has foregrounded the Communal Constitution, its model of the Indian people cohabits with the project to model the Indian people as a liberal community of equally free citizens. As repeatedly mentioned, this liberal vision is best associated with the moment leading up to the founding of the Indian republic and the manner in which this vision pervades the Constitution of independent India. The high tide of liberal political constitutionalism could be on the wane in the modern world as also in India, as noted earlier in this chapter. Nonetheless, it continues to be the background against which all alternatives of the Indian people are apprehended and appraised. Thus, in the scheme of this book, the Indian people understood as a liberal community and as a communal national community constitutes the principal axes around which sovereign power has been examined across the colonial and postcolonial periods.

On the other hand, identifying Indians along Chaterjee's axes of plurality and regional identity has been relatively less important to the discussions that have framed this book. Regional identity has been entirely peripheral to the concerns of this book. Though it has an older history, it is useful to flag the recognition of regional identity with the Constitution's incorporation of federal provinces set against the background of a strong central government. The bid to identify the Indian people with plural practice points to a civilisational dimension of Indian society that is best associated with the efforts of those like M. K. Gandhi who tried to draw a plurality of social practice into the efforts of nation building. This plurality of social and cultural practice is an important theme that arises in discussion across previous chapters, especially the chapters on minority rights and on the identification of castes groups. Even so, plurality as a dimension of constitutional identity was only cursorily discussed in Chapters 3 and 4. Thus, returning to accounts from plurality in this concluding section, it is possible to signal and speculate on its significance to apprehend and appraise the discussions in the previous chapters.

Plurality and the Indian People

Plurality was presented, especially in Chapters 3 and 4, as a form of social and perhaps even political belonging that challenged the dominance of communally, nationally, axiomatically, and doctrinally demarcated forms of identifying minorities and castes. Thus, of the different ways in which minorities were identified in Chapter 3, drawing on arguments from the framework of plurality, a term like 'Hindu' was argued for in judicial proceedings as part of a horizon of plural practice along which there could be no clear distinction between majorities and minorities. Alternatively, the term 'Hindu' was also argued for as an identity that demarcated a religious or national majority against which minority identities could be defined. Muslim identity was not discussed in either Chapter 3 or Chapter 4. However, the discussion on social reform in Chapter 2 suggests that Muslim identity could also be read similarly as part of a social plurality or, alternatively, as firmed up by legal design and practice as a distinct political identity. Thus, between these approaches, Chapter 3 presented a majoritarian imagination which sidelined communities that sought to present themselves along a spectrum of plural social practices in Indian constitutional practice.

Similarly, as discussed in Chapter 4, caste groups could be presented along sectarian and associational lines with a correspondingly greater recognition of plurality in the understanding of caste as a social phenomenon. That is, caste could be identified in ways that was not linked to or circumscribed by any one religious tradition. However, constitutional practice has consistently stuck with the account of caste as a social phenomenon tied together by a sacral account of the Hindu religion.

Thus, of the available ways of characterising social identities, state practice has for the most part cast Indian social identities through communal and national frames. By contrast, accounts from plurality highlight bottom-up and sociologically driven forms of political identification. Further, this account of the Indian people has had little place in the mainstream of discussions on Indian constitutional design and practice.[8] Of course, this is not to deny that both the communal-national and the liberal accounts of the Indian people have in differing degrees a reasonably well demarcated place for plurality and diversity. Thus, the Communal Constitution could recognise a diversity of communities in ways consistent with a nationalised conception of Hindu and Muslim identities. Thus, for example, the Communal Constitution would not be troubled by identities like the Ramakrishnas, the Swaminarayans and even the Jains as long as they could be subsumed within a larger nationalised conception of Hindu identity. Similarly, the liberal secular conception of the people could recognise diversity, even those associated with groups, so long as they were consistent with the equal liberty of citizens. However, as a distinct account of identification, arguments from plurality in Chapters 3 and 4 seem to present an important and entirely different approach to representing the sovereign power of the Indian people. That is, drawing on sociologically rooted civilisational diversity, these arguments from plurality represent an attempt to displace the centrality of sovereign state power that is implicit in both the Communal Constitution and the liberal secular account of the Indian Constitution.

Arguably, M. K. Gandhi is the best-known defender of this decentralised account of plurality – especially a defence of plurality understood as a space kept open for ethical practices through which individuals and social groups could explore the civilisational bonds that tied them to each other. Discussing either Gandhi's account of plural traditions of ethical practice or a broader account of civilisational plurality that engendered such practice is beyond the scope of this concluding comment.[9] However, it is possible to point to and suggest that important parts of Gandhi's thought drew on arguments from plurality to disarm the alienating effects of the modern condition, sovereign politics, as well as those aspects of communal identities that deeply troubled him.[10]

Drawing on *Hind Swaraj*, a pivotal restatement of Gandhi's political thought, scholars have pointed out that his criticism of modern industrial society was not the human advancement it brought about. On the contrary, the target of his attack was said to be the form in which the advances of modern society impeded the ability to engender ethical self-reflection which was at the heart of his idea of freedom, or *swaraj*.[11] Thus, key institutions and features of modern industrial society such as parliamentary democracy, lawyers, railways, medicines, and so on, were not attacked merely as emblems of modernity but as spaces that impeded *swaraj*.

Commenting in particular on Hindu traditions, he was always at pains to present the Hindu traditions as a far cry from 'exclusive nationalism' and the broader contours of sovereign state power that would view the Hindu ethical spectrum merely as a religious identity tied to sovereignty and state power.[12] As he put it, Hinduism was merely the civilisational background that structured a considerable part of ethical striving in South Asia. Therefore, being Hindu was cast as a 'search after the truth through non-violent means ... Hinduism is a relentless pursuit after truth.'[13] It followed that the Hindu traditions were not an identity or a people that authorised modern state power, but a space that facilitated individual self-making or *swaraj*.

Of course, even assuming a kernel of accuracy to this manner of characterising Gandhi's views about Hindu traditions, they could be dismissed as an idiosyncratic account of the tradition. Further, in the absence of a more detailed discussion, it is not possible to show that there is any necessary congruence between Gandhi's profound interest in delimiting Hindu practice as a space for truth-seeking and self-discovery and the claims of groups such as the Swaminarayans and even the Ramakrishna Mission whose self-presentation in earlier chapters permits this discussion on plurality. To the extent that the Swaminarayans sought to exclude members of other caste groups from their temples, it could be argued that they sought to defend practices that were far from ethical. However, to the extent that these traditions sought to decentre a nationally and axiomatically organised account of the Hindu traditions, Gandhi's Hinduism does map onto arguments echoing civilisational diversity that were presented by these groups as also in examples discussed in the cases across Chapters 3 and 4.

Thus, to the extent that Gandhi displaces nationalised, axiomatically, and doctrinally organised communal identities, he represents a novel way to draw on plurality to think about social identification and what it might mean to establish a politics based on the authority of a people. Further, to the extent that discussions in Chapters 3 and 4 map onto Gandhi's account of civilisational plurality, and of politics as a space for ethical self-reflection, they represent a novel way to consider the sovereign power of the people as it stands in relation to the existing contours of Indian constitutional design and practice.

Arguments drawn from plurality and diversity have not been examined in this book beyond the cursory form in which they are described in Chapters 3 and 4, and as they have been briefly examined in this concluding comment. This is clearly an aspect of this book's discussion that requires much more careful detailing and elaboration. Nonetheless, at a historical moment when the demand for a constitutional imagination that echoes Indic resources has never been stronger, it is important to note that this Gandhian approach to politics could offer important clues drawing on the authority of a people to authorise political power in diverse societies such as India.

The viability of plurality as a self-standing ground for authorising sovereign politics, or the manner in which plural practice could potentially be made consistent with the liberal secular state is a matter for separate enquiry.[14] However, as an offshoot of the Communal Constitution, these comments are only advanced as a preliminary attempt to flag the need for a more detailed and critical examination of arguments that flow from accounts drawn from plurality. On that note, tracing backwards to the core account of the Communal

Constitution that has framed this book, this chapter must now wind down with a short comment on the significance of the Communal Constitution for the normative project of defending liberal secular norms that have been repeatedly presented to be the bedrock that holds up the Constitution of independent India.

The Communal Constitution and Liberal Secular Ideals

The liberal secular norms of the Indian Constitution framed the efforts of this book to describe the lingering presence of the Communal Constitution. However, these norms were repeatedly bracketed from active examination to throw the contours of the Communal Constitution into sharper relief. Consequently, this concluding note now attempts to outline the significance of this account of the Communal Constitution for an understanding and defence of liberal secular norms.

As a primarily descriptive diagnostic and explanatory project, the Communal Constitution has no direct bearing on the defence of liberal secular norms. However, these contours of the Communal Constitution do have implications for understanding liberal norms as embodying an important though contested form of political community. As discussed earlier, contouring the Communal Constitution immediately brings to light the ecology of political projects that have sought to mould the Indian people in different ways. Of these, the liberal values of the Indian Constitution is only one among alternatives even if it is widely believed that it is best suited to address the challenge of managing diversity in modern societies.[15]

Liberal secular norms have with good reason been centrally associated with the founding values that underpin the Indian Constitution. However, from the perspective of this book, the foregrounding of these founding values without an awareness of their contested background has tended to shade out the broader constitutional field that shapes and cohabits with liberal values. In turn, this form of emphasising liberal values could also impede the effort to defend the aspirations at the heart of the Indian Constitution, as the following example will suggest.

Thus, consider the *Swaminarayan* case discussed in passing in Chapter 3. The case involved judicial examination of the constitutionality of a Bombay temple entry statute mandating that no section or class of Hindus could be excluded from a Hindu place of worship. Arguing that they were not Hindus, the Swaminarayans claimed immunity from the application of the statute to their temples. This in turn produced legal contest over the term 'Hindu', which has been discussed at greater length in Chapter 3. The contest over who is a Hindu could be mistaken merely as a normative issue bearing on legal interpretation of a statute. However, this book has tried to cast problems of this kind as a force-field that drew on religion and religious identification to frame the constitutional identity of the Indian people in very different ways.

Thus, Hindus understood as a religious community pulled together by doctrines drawn from texts like the Gita or the Vedas were presented as part of a nationalist account of the Indian people. By contrast, when described as part of a civilisational canvas of plural practices, the Hindu traditions were presented as an account of the Indian people that emphasised social diversity and plurality. As recounted in Chapters 1 and 3, much scholarship responds to this judicial approach to framing the dispute in this case as a failure of constitutional interpretation and not as a contest over constitutional identity. That is, important works of scholarship cast the efforts of the court as marked by a failure to defend the Constitution's liberal and reforming aspirations.[16]

Clearly, the effort to fathom correct or preferable answers to legal problems is an integral part of legal analysis. However, normative legal analysis is by definition an internal account of law and is often unable to make salient the broader social and political field in which legal problems takes shape. Thus, broadening the frame of analysis from the liberal legal ideas that animate the text of the Indian Constitution, this book has attempted to frame those legal norms as part of a broader, contested but nonetheless legal field engaged in carving out the identity of the Indian people.

More importantly, set against the liberal aspirations of the Indian Constitution, this book has also demonstrated a concerted constitutional slide or disposition to choose communal forms of identifying the Indian people in the debates outlined in previous chapters. Consequently, set against the contested field of characterising the Indian people, it is this slide towards communal forms of identifying the Indian people that presents the Communal Constitution as a pressing challenge for liberal constitutionalism as much as a phenomenon worthy of note and analysis.

Notes

1. For example, see Tom Ginsburg and Aziz Z. Huq, *How to Save a Constitutional Democracy* (1st edn, Chicago: University of Chicago Press, 2018); David Runciman, *How Democracy Ends* (New York: Basic Books, 2018); Chatterji, Hansen and Jaffrelot, *Majoritarian State*.

2. For example, Friedrich Engels and Karl Marx, 'On the Jewish Question' in *Marx–Engels Reader*, ed. Robert C Tucker, 26–53 (2nd edn, New York: W. W. Norton & Company, 1978).

3. For an overview of this body of scholarship, see Udi Greenberg and Daniel Steinmetz-Jenkins, 'Introduction', *Journal of the American Academy of Religion* 88, no. 1 (2020): 1; Loughlin, 'On Constituent Power'.

4. For example, see Upendra Baxi, 'Constitutionalism as a Site of State Formative Practices', *Cardozo Law Review* 21 (1999): 1183; Upendra Baxi, 'The (Im)Possibility of Constitutional Justice: Seismographic Notes on Indian Constitutionalism' in *India's Living Constitution: Ideas, Practices, Controversies*, ed. Zoya Hasan and R. Sudarshan, 31–63 (New Delhi: Permanent Black, 2002).

5. For example, see Bhatia, *The Transformative Constitution*.

6. For example, see Khosla, *India's Founding Moment*.

7. Chatterjee, *The Nation and Its Fragments*, 76–115.

8. See, for example, the discussion ruling out the possibility of actively organising the Indian Constitutional to embody Gandhian values in Austin, *The Indian Constitution*, 39–41.

9. For example, see Vivek Dhareshwar, 'Politics, Experience and Cognitive Enslavement: Gandhi's Hind Swaraj', *Economic and Political Weekly* 45, no. 12 (2010): 51; Akeel Bilgrami, 'Gandhi, the Philosopher', *Economic and Political Weekly* 38, no, 39 (2003): 4159, http://www.epw.in/special-articles/gandhi-philosopher.html, accessed 3 December 2015.

10. I have tried to outline this problem previously in Mathew John, 'Social Intuitions in the Shadow of Liberal Constitutionalism: A Perspective from Indian Constitutional Law', *Constitutionalism Beyond Liberalism*, ed. Michael W. Dowdle and Michael A. Wilkinson, 129–47 (Cambridge, UK: Cambridge University Press, 2017).

11. Bilgrami, 'Gandhi, the Philosopher'; Dhareshwar, 'Politics, Experience and Cognitive Enslavement'.

12. Sabyasachi Bhattacharya, *Mahatma and the Poet: Letters and Debates Between Gandhi and Tagore 1915–1941* (1st edn, New Delhi: National Book Trust, 1997), 30.

13. Mahatma Gandhi, *Hindu Dharma* (New Delhi: Orient Paperbacks, 1978), 18–19.

14. Salmoli Choudhuri's account of Tagore is a useful example to think of this problem. As a close interlocutor of Gandhi as well as being a staunch critic of nationalism himself, the manner in which Tagore is explored here throws light on the lines of enquiry that accounts about plurality must tread to

explore its implications a novel form of authorising the political power of a people. Salmoli Choudhuri, 'Theology of the "Absent King" and the Possibility of Rabindranath Tagore's Political Thought', *Political Theology* 23, nos. 1–2 (2022): 44.

15. See, however, scholarship on relational constituent power in Loughlin (n 5); Martin Loughlin, *Foundations of Public Law* (Reprint edn, Oxford: Oxford University Press, 2010).

16. Bhatia, 'Freedom from Community'.

Bibliography

Cases

Abdul Kadir v. Dharma 20 Bom. 190 (1895).

Arya Samaj Education Trust, Delhi v. The Director of Education AIR 1976 Delhi 207.

Bal Patil & Anr. v. Union of India MANU/SC/0472/2005.

Bramchari Sidheswar Bhai v. State of West Bengal MANU/SC/0413/1995.

Chitturbhuj Vithaldas Jasani v. Moreshwar Parashram & Ors 1954 AIR 236.

D. A. V. College v. State of Punjab 1971(2)SCC 269.

Durgah Committee; Ajmer and Anr. v. Syed Hussain Ali and Ors. MANU/SC/0063/1961.

Gopal Singh Visharad and Others v. Zahoor Ahmad and Others MANU/UP/1185/2010.

Harvinder Kaur v. Harminder Singh AIR 1984 Del 66.

Hindu Religious Endowments, Madras v. Sri Laxmindra Thirtha Swamiar of Shirur Mutt MANU/SC/0136/1954.

Indian Young Lawyers Association v. State of Kerala MANU/SC/1094/2018.

Indra Sawhney v. Union of India MANU/SC/0104/1993.

Ismail Faruqui v. Union of India MANU/SC/0126/1995.

Ismail Faruqui v. UOI MANU/SC/0860/1994.

Jagdishwaranand v. Police Commissioner, Calcutta MANU/SC/0050/1983.

John Vallamattom v. Union of India, 6 SCC 611 (2003).

Jordan Diengdeh v. S.S. Chopra AIR 1985 SC 935.

Jose Paulo Coutinho v. Maria Luiza Valentina Pereira (2019) SCC ONLINE SC 1190.

K. P. Manu v. Chairman, Scrutiny Committee for Verification of Community Certificate MANU/SC/0189/2015.

Kailash Sonkar v. Maya Devi (1984) 2 SCC 91.

Kattalai Michael Pillai and Ors. v. Right Reverend J. M. Barthe, S. J. Bishop of Trichinopoly and Ors. AIR 1917 Mad 431.

M Siddiq v. Mahant Suresh Das MANU/SC/1538/2019.

M.H. Qureshi v. State of Bihar MANU/SC/0027/1958.

M.R.Balaji v. State of Mysore AIR 1963 SC 649.

Madura v. Mootoo Ramalinga 12 M.I.A. 397 (1868).

Mohd. Ahmed Khan v. Shah Bano Begam MANU/SC/0194/1985.

Nikhil Soni v. Union of India 2015.

Pramati Educational & Cultural Trust & Ors. v. Union of India (2014) 8 SCC 1.

Principal Guntur v. Mohan Rao (1976) 3 SCC 411.

Rev. Sidhajbhai Sabhai and Ors. v. State of Bombay, [1963] 3 SCR 837.

S. Anbalagan v. B. Devarajan & Ors (1984) 2 SCC 112.

S. Rajagopal v. C. M. Armugam AIR 1969 SC 101.

S.P. Mittal v. Union of India AIR MANU/SC/0532/1982.

Sarla Mudgal v. Union of India MANU/SC/0290/1995.

Saroj Rani v. Sudarshan AIR 1984 SC 1562l.

Sastri Yagnapurushadji v. Muldas Bhudardas Vaishya MANU/SC/0040/1966.

Shayara Bano v. Union of India and Ors. MANU/SC/1031/2017.

Soosai v. Union of India MANU/SC/0045/1985.

St. Xavier College v. State of Gujarat AIR 1974 SC 1389.

State of Bombay v. Narasu Appa Mali MANU/MH/0040/1952.

State of Madras v. Champakam Dorairajan AIR 1951 SC 226.

Tilkayat Tilkayat Shri Govindlalji Maharaj v. State of Rajastan MANU/SC/0028/1963.

TMA Pai v. State of Karnataka (2002)8 SCC 481.

Venkataramana Devaru v. State of Mysore 1958 AIR 255.

Books, Chapters and Articles

Agnes, F. 'Hindu Men, Monogamy and Uniform Civil Code'. *Economic and Political Weekly* 30, no. 50 (1995): 3238.

———. 'Has the Codified Hindu Law Changed Gender Relationships?' *Social Change* 46, no. 4 (2016): 611.

Anderson, M. 'Islamic Law and the Colonial Encounter'. In *Institutions and Ideologies: A SOAS South Asia Reader*, edited by David Arnold and Peter Robb, 165–85. London: Routledge, 1993.

Ansari, I. 'Minorities and the Politics of Constitution Making in India'. In *Minority Identities and the Nation-state*, edited by D. Sheth and Gurpreet Mahajan, 113–37. New Delhi: Oxford University Press, 1999.

Asif, M. A. *The Loss of Hindustan: The Invention of India*. Cambridge, MA: Harvard University Press, 2020.

Austin, G. *The Indian Constitution: Cornerstone of a Nation*. New Delhi: Oxford University Press, 1966.

Bajpai, R. *Debating Difference: Group Rights and Liberal Democracy in India*. Oxford: Oxford University Press, 2011.

Baxi, U. 'Constitutionalism as a Site of State Formative Practices'. *Cardozo Law Review* 21 (1999): 1183.

———. 'The (Im)Possibility of Constitutional Justice: Seismographic Notes on Indian Constitutionalism'. In *India's Living Constitution: Ideas, Practices, Controversies*, edited by Zoya Hasan and R. Sudarshan, 31–63. New Delhi: Permanent Black, 2002.

Béteille, André. *The Backward Classes in Contemporary India*. Delhi: Oxford University Press 1992.

Bhatia, G. 'Freedom from Community: Individual Rights, Group Life, State Authority and Religious Freedom under the Indian Constitution'. *Global Constitutionalism* 5, no. 3 (2016): 351.

———. 'The Supreme Court's Triple Talaq Judgment'. *Indian Constitutional Law and Philosophy*, 22 August 2017. https://indconlawphil.wordpress.com/2017/08/22/the-supreme-courts-triple-talaq-judgment/, accessed 10 December 2021.

———. *The Transformative Constitution: A Radical Biography in Nine Acts*. New Delhi: HarperCollins India, 2019.

Bhattacharya, S. *Mahatma and the Poet: Letters and Debates Between Gandhi and Tagore 1915–1941*. 1st edn, New Delhi: National Book Trust, 1997.

Bilgrami, A. 'Gandhi, the Philosopher'. *Economic and Political Weekly* 38, no. 39 (2003): 4159–65. http://www.epw.in/special-articles/gandhi-philosopher.html, accessed 3 December 2015.

Brown, J. M. *Modern India: The Origins of an Asian Democracy*. Oxford: Oxford University Press, 1985.

Carroll, L. 'Law, Custom, and Statutory Social Reform: The Hindu Widows' Remarriage Act of 1856'. *Indian Economic and Social History Review* 20, no. 4 (1983): 363.

Chakrabarthy, D. 'Postcoloniality and the Artifice of History: Who Speaks for "Indian" Pasts?' *Representations* 37 (Winter 1992): 1.

Chandra, A. 'Gopal Singh Visharad and Ors V. Zahoor Ahmad and Ors., O.S.Nos. 1/1989, 3/1989, 4/1989, 5/1989: A Summary of the Babri Masjid-Ram Janm

Bhoomi Decision'. (2010) SSRN eLibrary, http://papers.ssrn.com/sol3/papers.cfm?abstract_id=1690803, accessed 17 February 2011.

Char, S. V. D. (ed.). *Readings in the Constitutional History of India 1757–1947.* New Delhi: Oxford University Press, 1983.

Charsley, S. '"Untouchable": What Is in a Name?' *Journal of the Royal Anthropological Institute* 2, no. 1 (1996): 1

Chatterjee, P. *The Nation and Its Fragments.* New Delhi: Oxford University Press, 1995.

———. 'Secularism and Tolerance'. In *Secularism and Its Critics,* edited by Rajeev Bhargava. New Delhi: Oxford University Press, 1999.

Chatterji, A. P., Hansen, T. B. and Jaffrelot, C. (eds.). *Majoritarian State: How Hindu Nationalism Is Changing India.* London: C Hurst & Co Publishers Ltd, 2019.

Chiriyankandath, J. '"Democracy" under the Raj: Elections and Separate Representation in British India'. *Journal of Commonwealth and Comparative Politics* 30, no. 1 (1992): 39.

Choudhuri, S. 'Theology of the "Absent King" and the Possibility of Rabindranath Tagore's Political Thought'. *Political Theology* 23, nos. 1–2 (2022): 44.

Cohn, B. S. *Colonialism and Its Forms of Knowledge: The British in India.* Princeton: Princeton University Press, 1996.

———. 'Law and the Colonial State in India'. In *Colonialism and Its Forms of Knowledge: The British in India.* Princeton: Princeton: Princeton University Press, 1996.

'Constituent Assembly Debates'. https://www.constitutionofindia.net/constitution_assembly_debates/volume/7/1948-11-23, accessed 9 December 2021.

Constituent Assembly Debates: Official Report, vol 4. New Delhi: Lok Sabha Secretariat, 1999.

———. vol 7. New Delhi: Lok Sabha Secretariat 1999.

———. vol 5. New Delhi: Lok Sabha Secretariat 1999.

———. vol 10. New Delhi: Lok Sabha Secretariat 1999.

———. vol 9. New Delhi: Lok Sabha Secretariat 1999.

Coupland, R., *Report on the Constitutional Problem in India: The Indian Problem, 1833–1935.* Oxford: Oxford University Press, 1943.

Davis, D. R. *The Spirit of Hindu Law.* Reprint edn, Cambridge, UK: Cambridge University Press, 2013.

De, R. 'Constitutional Antecedents'. In *The Oxford Handbook of the Indian Constitution,* edited by Pratap Bhanu Mehta, Madhav Khosla and Sujit Choudhry, 17–38. New Delhi: Oxford University Press, 2016.

De Roover, J. and Balagangadhara, S. N., 'Liberty Tyranny and the Will of God: The Principle of Toleration in Early Modern Europe and Colonial India'. *History of Political Thought* 30, no. 1 (2009): 111.

Derrett, J. D. M. 'J. H. Nelson: A Forgotten Administrator-Historian of India'. In *Historians of India, Pakistan and Ceylon*, ed. Cyril Henry Philips, 354–72. Oxford: Oxford University Press, 1961.

———. 'The British as Patrons of the Sastra'. In *Religion, Law and the State in India*, edited by J. D. M. Derrett, 225–74. New Delhi: Oxford University Press, 1999.

Dhareshwar, V. 'Politics, Experience and Cognitive Enslavement: Gandhi's Hind Swaraj'. *Economic and Political Weekly* 45, no. 12 (2010): 51.

Dhavan, R. and Nariman, F. S. 'The Supreme Court and Group Life: Religious Freedom, Minority Groups and Disadvantaged Communities'. In *Supreme but Not Infallible: Essays in Honour of the Supreme Court of India*, edited by B. N. Kirpal and Ashok H. Desai, 256–89. New Delhi: Oxford University Press, 2000.

Dirks, N. B., 'Castes of Mind'. *Representations* 37 (Winter 1992): 56.

———. *Castes of Mind: Colonialism and the Making of Modern India.* New Delhi: Permanent Black, 2003.

'East India (Advisory and Legislative Councils, &c.). Vol. I. Proposals of the Government of India and Despatch of the Secretary of State.' (1908). http://gateway.proquest.com/openurl?url_ver=Z39.88-2004&res_dat=xri:hcpp&rft_dat=xri:hcpp:rec:1908-010247, accessed 24 April 2022.

Engels, F. and Marx, K. 'On the Jewish Question'. In *Marx–Engels Reader*, edited by Robert C. Tucker, 26–52. 2nd edn, New York: W W Norton & Company, 1978.

Galanter, M. 'Religious Aspects of Caste'. In *South Asian Politics and Religion*, edited by Donald Eugene Smith, 277–310. Princeton: Princeton University Press, 1966.

———. *Competing Equality: Law and the Backword Classes in India.* Berkeley: University of California Press, 1984.

Gandhi, M. *Hindu Dharma.* New Delhi: Orient Paperbacks, 1978.

Geetha, V. and Rajadurai, S. V. *Towards a Non-Brahmin Millennium: From Iyothee Thass to Periyar.* Calcutta: Samya, 1998.

Ghosh, P. S. *The Politics of Personal Law in South Asia: Identity, Nationalism and the Uniform Civil Code.* Routledge India, 2007.

Ginsburg, T. and Huq, A. Z. *How to Save a Constitutional Democracy.* 1st edn, Chicago: University of Chicago Press, 2018.

Gopal, S. *British Policy in India, 1858–1905.* Cambridge, UK: Cambridge University Press, 1965.

Greenberg, U. and Steinmetz-Jenkins, D. 'Introduction'. *Journal of the American Academy of Religion* 88, no. 1 (2020): 1

Innes, L. C. *Examination of Mr. Nelson's Views of Hindu Law, in a Letter to the Right Hon. Mountstuart Elphinstone Grant Duff, Governor of Madras*. Madras: Higginbotham & Co, 1882.

Jenkins, L. D. *Identity and Identification in India*. London: Routledge, 2003.

John, M. 'Framing Religion in Constitutional Politics: A View from Indian Constitutional Law'. *South Asian History and Culture* 10, no. 2 (2019): 124–35.

———. 'Parochialism in Indian Constitutional Reasoning: The Case of Religious Freedom'. *Verfassung und Recht in Übersee/Law and Politics in Africa, Asia and Latin America* 51, no. 3 (2018) 332–51.

———. 'Social Intuitions in the Shadow of Liberal Constitutionalism: A Perspective from Indian Constitutional Law'. *Constitutionalism Beyond Liberalism*, edited by M. W. Dowdle and M. A. Wilkinson, 129–47. Cambridge, UK: Cambridge University Press, 2017.

Jones, K. W. *Socio-Religious Reform Movements in British India*. New Delhi: Cambridge University Press, 1994.

Khosla, M. *India's Founding Moment – The Constitution of a Most Surprising Democracy*. Cambridge, MA: Harvard University Press, 2020.

Kozlowski, G. C. *Muslim Endowments and Society in British India*. Cambridge, UK: Cambridge University Press, 2008.

Kymlicka, W. *Liberalism, Community and Culture*. Oxford: Oxford University Press, 1989.

Lariviere, R.W. 'Justices and Panditas: Some Ironies in Contemporary Readings of the Hindu Legal Past'. *The Journal of Asian Studies* 48, no. 4 (1989): 757.

Lingat, R. *The Classical Law of India*. New edn, New Delhi: Oxford University Press, 1998.

Loughlin, M. *Foundations of Public Law*. Reprint edn, Oxford: Oxford University Press, 2010.

———. 'On Constituent Power'. In *Constitutionalism beyond Liberalism*, edited by M. W. Dowdle and M. A. Wilkinson, 151–75. Cambridge, UK: Cambridge University Press, 2017.

Macaulay, T. B. 'Government of India'. *Miscellaneous Writings and Speeches*, vol. 4 (Project Gutenberg 2008). https://www.gutenberg.org/files/2170/2170-h/2170-h.htm, accessed 8 November 2022.

Madan, T. N. *Modern Myths, Locked Minds: Secularism and Fundamentalism in India*. 2nd edn, New Delhi: Oxford University Press, 2009.

Mahmood, T. *Uniform Civil Code: Fictions and Facts*. New Delhi: India and Islam Research Council, 1995.

Major, A. *Pious Flames: European Encounters with Sati 1500–1830*. New Delhi: Oxford University Press, 2006.

Mallampalli, C. *Race, Religion and Law in Colonial India: Trials of an Interracial Family*. Cambridge: Cambridge University Press, 2011.

Mani, L. 'Contentious Traditions: The Debate on Sati in Colonial India'. In *Recasting Women: Essays in Indian Colonial History*, edited by Kumkum Sangari and Sudesh Vaid, 88–126. New Delhi: Kali for Women, 1989.

Mayne, J. D. *A Treatise on Hindu Law and Usage.* 7th ed., Higginbotham & Co, 1906.

Mehta, P. B. 'Hinduism and Self-Rule'. *Journal of Democracy* 15, no. 3 (2004): 108–21.

———. 'On the Possibility of Religious Pluralism'. In *Religious Pluralism, Globalization, and World Politics*, edited by Thomas Banchoff, 65–88. New York: Oxford University Press, 2008.

Mehta, U. S. *Liberalism and Empire: India in British Liberal Thought.* New Delhi: Oxford University Press, 1999.

———. 'Constitutionalism'. In *The Oxford Companion to Politics in India*, edited by Niraja Gopal Jayal and Pratap Bhanu Mehta, 15–27. New Delhi: Oxford University Press, 2010.

Menski, W. 'The Uniform Civil Code Debate in Indian Law: New Developments and Changing Agenda'. *German Law Journal* 9, no. 3 (2008): 211.

Misra, R. 'Report of the National Commission for Religious and Linguistic Minorities'. Ministry of Minority Affairs, 2007. https://www.sabrangindia. in/reports/2007-delhi-report-national-commission-religious-and-linguistic-minorities-ranganath-misra, accessed 8 November 2022.

Mitter, D. N. *Position of Women in Hindu Law*, vol. 1. New Delhi: Cosmo Publications, 2006.

Morley, J. *Indian Speeches (1907–1909).* London: Macmillan, 1909.

Nandy, A., Shikha Trivedy, Shail Mayaram and Achyut Yagnik. *Creating a Nationality: The Ramjanmabhumi Movement and Fear of the Self.* New Delhi: Oxford University Press, 1998.

Nelson, J. H. *A View of the Hindu Law as Administered by the High Court of Judicature at Madras.* Madras: Higginbotham & Co., 1877.

———. *A Prospectus of the Scientific Study of the Hindû Law.* London: Kegan Paul & Co, 1881.

———. *Indian Usage and Judge Made Law in Madras.* London: Kegan Paul & Co, 1887.

Newbigin, E. 'The Codification of Personal Law and Secular Citizenship'. *Indian Economic and Social History Review* 46, no. 1 (2009): 83.

Noorani, A. G. *The Babri Masjid Question, 1528–2003: 'A Matter of National Honour'*, vol. 1. New Delhi: Tulika Books, 2004)

Palshikar, S. 'Challenges before the Reservation Discourse'. *Economic and Political Weekly* 43, no. 9 (200): 8.

Pathan, S. 'A Historical and Theoretical Investigation into Communalism'. Thesis Submitted to Manipal University, 2009.

Prasanna Kumar, A. 'Uniform Civil Code: A Heedless Quest?' *Economic and Political Weekly* 51, no. 25 (2015): 7.

Purohit, T. *The Aga Khan Case: Religion and Identity in Colonial India.* Sew edn, Cambridge, MA: Harvard University Press, 2012.

Radhakrishnan, S. *Indian Philosophy*, vol. 1. London: George Allen and Unwin Ltd, 1948.

Rankin, G. 'Custom and the Muslim Law in British India'. *Transactions of the Grotius Society* 25 (1939): 89.

Rao, B. S., et al. *The Framing of India's Constitution*, vol. 2. New Delhi: Indian Institute of Public Administration, 1966.

———. *The Framing of India's Constitution*, vol. 4. New Delhi: Indian Institute of Public Administration, 1966.

Rawls, J. *Political Liberalism.* New York: Columbia University Press, 2005.

Reddy, K. V. 'Minority Educational Institutions'. In *The Oxford Handbook of the Indian Constitution*, edited by Sujit Choudhry, Madhav Khosla and Pratap Bhanu Mehta, 921–942. New Delhi: Oxford University Press, 2016.

'Report on Indian Constitutional Reform'. Calcutta: Superintendent Government of India Press, 1918.

Roover, J. D. *Europe, India, and the Limits of Secularism.* New Delhi: Oxford University Press, 2015.

Runciman, D. *How Democracy Ends.* New York: Basic Books, 2018.

Sangai, A., A. Gaur, A. Sengupta and S. Ambasht. 'Right to Education and Minority Rights: Towards a Fine Constitutional Balance'. New Delhi: Vidhi Centre for Legal Policy, 2016.

Seervai, H. M. *Constitutional Law of India*, vol. 2. 4th edn, Bombay: Universal Law Publishing – An imprint of LexisNexis, 2015.

Sen, R. *Articles of Faith: Religion, Secularism and Indian Supreme Court.* New Delhi: Oxford University Press, 2010.

Shodhan, A. *A Question of Community: Religious Groups and Colonial Law.* Calcutta: Samya, 2001.

Sinha, C. *Debating Patriarchy: The Hindu Code Bill Controversy in India.* New Delhi: Oxford University Press, 2012.

Sitapati, V. 'Reservations'. In *The Oxford Handbook of the Indian Constitution*, edited by Sujit Choudhry, Madhav Khosla and Pratap Bhanu Mehta, 720–41. New Delhi: Oxford University Press, 2016.

Smith, D. E. *India as a Secular State.* Princeton: Princeton University Press, 1963.

Srikantan, G. 'Reexamining Secularism'. *Journal of Law, Religion and State* 5, no. 2 (2017): 117.

———. *Identifying and Regulating Religion in India: Law, History and the Place of Worship.* New Delhi: Cambridge University Press, 2020.

Srivastava, S. 'How the British Saw the Issue'. In *Anatomy of a Confrontation : The Babri Masjid-Ramjanmabhumi Issue*, edited by Sarvepalli Gopal, 38–57. New Delhi; New York, NY: Penguin Books, 1991.

Sullivan, W. F. *The Impossibility of Religious Freedom*. Princeton: Princeton University Press, 2007.

Surendranath, A. 'Essential Practices Doctrine: Towards Inevitable Constitutional Burial'. *Journal of the National Human Rights Commission, India* 15 (2016): 159.

The Nehru Report: An Anti-Separatist Manifesto. New Delhi: Michiko & Panjathan, under the auspices of the Indian Institute of Applied Political Research, 1975.

Williams, R. V. *Postcolonial Politics and Personal Laws: Colonial Legal Legacies and the Indian State*. New Delhi: Oxford University Press, 2006.

Zelliot, E. M., 'Dr. Ambedkar and the Mahar Movement'. University of Pennsylvania, 1969. https://repository.upenn.edu/dissertations/AAI6921466, accessed 8 November 2022.

Index